How to Master Your Medical School Finals

How to Master Your Medical School Finals

The complete guide to passing and excelling in your medical school exams

Dr Robert Tan and
Dr Christopher See

KoganPage

LONDON PHILADELPHIA NEW DELHI

First published in Great Britain in 2011 by Kogan Page Limited

120 Pentonville Road
London N1 9JN
United Kingdom
www.koganpage.com

© Robert Tan and Christopher See, 2011

The right of Robert Tan and Christopher See to be identified as the authors of this work has been asserted by them in accordance with the Copyright, Designs and Patents Act 1988.

ISBN   978 0 7494 6353 3
E-ISBN   978 0 7494 6357 1

British Library Cataloguing-in-Publication Data

A CIP record for this book is available from the British Library.

Typeset by Graphicraft Limited, Hong Kong
Print production managed by Jellyfish
Printed in the UK by CPI Antony Rowe

Contents

Introduction

Learning factual information is something which medical students are generally very good at. Large medical reference books, lecture notes and online resources are read and digested on a day-to-day basis. However, these books cannot tell you how to pass an exam. They do not tell you about the common mistakes of students, what makes a student excel, which conditions are more likely to appear in OSCE situations, how to prepare for MCQ's or what to do with your time in medical school to get the most out of it. We distil all those handy tips and tricks that get handed down during bedside teaching and informal teaching sessions. We wanted to provide a student with the means and tools to maximize their time in any given teaching opportunity, to have confidence in responding to any verbal or written question, and to perform a slick examination and presentation of findings.

This book will act as your 'pocket supervisor', showing you how to develop your skills and increase your knowledge as you progress through medical school. Preparation for finals starts in your first year, and unlike other books, we will guide you through your clinical years.

Rather than focus on delivering basic knowledge, we improve the process by which you acquire new knowledge and skills. Once you have the level of knowledge and skills required to pass, we provide tips on how to consolidate them, and show you how to deliver a slick clinical examination and distinction-level written or verbal answer.

We discuss learning strategies tailored to specific clinical environments such as general wards, clinic and theatre, enabling you to get the most out of any learning opportunity and to build a productive day in hospital.

We explode the myth that you have to be a genius to get a distinction or a merit award. We point out the areas to focus on for those extra marks, and tell you how to deliver a well-structured, concise and eloquent answer.

There is a chapter detailing a unique approach to each of the core specialties of paediatrics, surgery, obstetrics and gynaecology, pathology and psychiatry. We discuss the key topics for each, along with a specialty specific history and examination section.

We also show you how to analyse your own learning style and how to incorporate new methods of learning. We discuss ways to consolidate and build on material you have already learnt to enable rapid recall.

Taking you through a step-by-step approach to the last six months before finals, we have included advice on how to construct a reliable revision timetable, what to save as last minute reading, and an invaluable list of last minute revision topics.

There are hundreds of books showing you how to perform a perfect examination, but none that highlight common mistakes, examiner preferences and tips to make it look like you have examined thousands of patients before!

We shine a light into the depths of OSCE finals, giving you a system to approach the more unusual OSCE's such as blood transfusions and prescription errors. We also provide guidance on how to approach a communication skills station, and which principles to use when navigating challenging scenarios such as angry patients or breaking bad news.

There are many different ways to practice your examination skills and we discuss the use of simulated patients, mannequins and real patients and what each can offer.

An entire chapter is dedicated to teaching you how to answer a question thrown at you on a ward round or in an OSCE. We analyse different types of question and provide 20 worked examples to show you how to deliver a distinction-level answer.

Many students find it difficult to learn imaging in a systematic format. We provide several different methods for each of the main types of imaging commonly used. The student is then taken through basic and advanced techniques of presenting the results of imaging.

We provide an unbiased review of the core textbooks for each specialty in an effort to assist a student in the decision about which books to buy (and which to borrow from a library).

The online memory audit is a new concept to most students, and provides a structure upon which the endless facts can be placed. This tool will help you to find out how much you still do not know; the first step of the path to passing finals.

Students often lament that they don't know how much detail is expected of each condition covered on the course. We provide a sample curriculum for medicine and surgery in an effort to provide some guidance on how to divide your time in the approach to finals.

There are subtleties to the art of MCQ and EMQ papers that we will discuss in an effort to improve the way you prepare for and sit these exams. From question structure to different methods of tackling MCQ questions to question spotting, we show you how to excel in your written exams.

Medical ethics and law is now examined in various forms in every medical school. We will take you through the main topics in a clear style, including landmark cases, legislature and ethical issues, as well as the often neglected clinical issues which will help demonstrate your understanding.

PART ONE

Preparation

CHAPTER 1

Maximizing time in hospital

This chapter aims to increase your productivity by improving the quality of time spent in hospital. It is easy to spend an entire day in hospital attending ward rounds, radiology meetings and clinics and helping out the on-call doctor while simultaneously failing to learn anything useful for finals. The hospital comprises many different areas, each unique in what it can offer in terms of learning, and this chapter gives advice on how to approach each area in a focused manner.

Ward rounds

These may be of direct educational value but time is usually limited, so teaching is sometimes neglected. Your priorities should include making a note of patients with classic presentations or interesting signs, presenting cases to the registrar and learning from foundation doctors who have recently taken finals. Broadly speaking, there are usually three types of ward round, categorized by who 'leads' it. The general approach by clinicians of different seniority is outlined below and is a result of their knowledge, experience and the pressures on their time.

Consultant led

These ward rounds tend to be brief, slick and to the point. The amount of teaching varies hugely and is mostly dependent on the individual consultant in terms of the importance they place on teaching. They also have more pressures on their time, such as the need to get to clinic, the endoscopy suite or theatre.

If you are not invited to answer questions or examine patients on the round, then it is reasonable to ask a few questions to remind everyone that it is a teaching hospital and you need to be taught. However, be aware of the balance that needs to be struck, and that too many questions will undoubtedly slow an already pressured ward round and the team will not thank you for holding things up.

On a more mundane, paperwork note, it is also very important to be present on a weekly basis as the consultant will be 'signing' you off at the end of the attachment and needs to have seen you on their ward round (as well as in their clinics and at bronchoscopy, endoscopy, etc).

> I try to make my presence felt on the consultant rounds by asking questions frequently. Then the consultant can remember me when it comes to the end-of-attachment sign-off.
>
> PA, fifth-year medical student

Registrar led

These rounds are usually relatively quick, with occasional pauses to ask students a question or two. You should try to take advantage of the registrar's detailed knowledge and possibly the most up-to-date practice in terms of current best evidence. One way to access this might be to clerk one of the new patients who arrives on the ward and then present them to the registrar. This is helpful to the registrar, who can use your history and examination as a basis on which to perform an abbreviated assessment of the patient. You have most to gain in the discussion which follows regarding your plan for the investigation and early management of the patient. This is a great opportunity to present the results of imaging, such as chest radiographs, ECGs, blood gases and CT head scans to a senior clinician, much like you might do in finals (for tips on learning and presenting imaging, see Chapter 10).

Foundation/core trainee led

These rounds tend to be the slowest but present the best opportunity to ask questions. The doctor or trainee will be extremely grateful for any help you can offer in terms of filling in request cards, venepuncture and writing up the patient's notes, but be careful to get all of these countersigned by a registered doctor.

Foundation-year doctors are an invaluable resource with regards to finals. You should ask them which cases they had in their final exams and whether they recommend any additional local resources; for example, many district general hospitals offer their own set of teaching sessions. These vary hugely between hospitals and also between departments, but the doctor may particularly recommend a specific set of teaching sessions given by a consultant who is an excellent teacher.

> I asked every foundation doctor which cases they had in their finals, and if they found a particular set of revision lectures helpful.
>
> TP, recent graduate

If the doctor graduated from your medical school, make sure you ask them if there are any commonly recurring patient groups in finals, usually as a result of having several families in the local area who suffer from the same inherited condition, such as neurofibromatosis or Von Hippel–Lindau syndrome. Find out if your tertiary hospital holds specialist clinics for rare diseases such as myasthenia gravis, systemic sclerosis or Marfan's syndrome, from which patients are often recruited for final examinations. The doctor may recall preferences on the part of the examiners regarding the style of physical examination or presentation of examination findings.

Foundation-year doctors have only recently been through the same examination process as you are facing and are an excellent resource of recently examined objective structured clinical examination (OSCE) cases, examiner preferences and pet hates.

KEY POINTS

- If a patient has been identified to you by the team as being good to examine, introduce yourself and ask their permission for you to return later to examine them.
- Most wards get a few new patients every day, so take the opportunity to clerk them and present to the team. If you continue to do this for a whole week you will quickly become familiar with most of the 20 to 30 patients on a general ward.
- Both the registrar and foundation doctor are well placed to advise you which patients have good signs or an interesting history.
- Help out the foundation-year 1 or 2 with odd jobs as the round progresses, which will make you feel part of the team, make the team better disposed to you and buy them more time to go over any interesting points raised during the round.
- Ask a keen foundation-year doctor, core trainee or registrar to go over a topic, examination or case as often as possible and you may be pleasantly surprised at their willingness to teach.

I often found that impromptu teaching given by a keen junior doctor was more finals-relevant than formal teaching given by a consultant.

- *Don't* waste your time doing endless ward jobs which have no learning value if the team is not repaying the favour by discussing interesting cases or watching you examine or listening to you present your findings.

RW, foundation-year doctor

General wards

Wards are full of patients with excellent histories and signs. Liaise with your friends and between several of you compile a list of patients that have good signs to examine. Patients often have a lot of spare time waiting for investigations or treatments, and are likely to be willing for you to perform a full examination of the relevant system.

Ensure you bear in mind those times of the day which are 'protected' patient time, ie team ward rounds, lunchtime and visiting times for relatives. Also be understanding to those patients who have already been examined by several of your colleagues earlier that day. Don't forget that these patients are often very unwell, and despite this are making a special effort to allow you to examine them. Therefore you should never press them if they aren't happy to be examined, and while examining them or standing around the bedside you should always be very gentle and respectful.

Always remember:

- *Don't* just stroll into a patient's room, ask to examine them and then be surprised and upset that they refuse.

- *Do* correctly identify the patient from the ward patient board (usually by the main nursing station), politely introduce yourself as you enter, engage them in conversation regarding how they are feeling and gently ask if they would mind you either taking a history or examining them. Once you have built a rapport with the patient you will have a much lower failure rate.

I always had a little chat with the patient about general topics before politely asking if they minded me examining them. I very rarely got refused using this approach.

MM, core trainee in surgery

Meetings

There are several meetings which take place every week, including ward-based types such as the 'discharge planning', which involves the occupational therapist, physiotherapist, nurse in charge and the lead consultant. There are other hospital-based meetings such as radiology or oncology meetings.

There is an increasing expectation that students understand the precise roles and services offered by these teams, and rightly so, as they are often indispensible when trying to facilitate patient discharge. Your role in these meetings is minimal, perhaps limited to writing patient notes about the plans discussed. Use the time to understand how the services are structured and operate.

A well-taken history in your OSCEs may unearth some mobility difficulties or concerns about increased social support which you can seek to address in your answer by including the above teams in your management plan.

There is generally little need to attend these every single week, and the team will hopefully understand if you attend the first few and then use the time for private study or to examine patients elsewhere.

> Be a good team player and focus on your 'home ward' for the first couple of weeks, attending any meetings and most ward rounds. Once you understand the structure and dynamics of the team and have sat in on a few meetings, the team should be happy if you want to go and read in the library or examine patients on another ward instead of attending your third discharge planning meeting.

Radiology, trauma or oncology MDT meetings

These can sometimes be frantic, especially multidisciplinary team (MDT) meetings such as oncology, but in the others there may be an attempt to include the medical students and you can expect the first line of questions to come your way.

Once you get over the initial anxiety about voicing your opinions in a room full of senior doctors, this is a great place to learn from a large group of experienced clinicians.

Take special note of the way cases are presented in a concise manner, and which information is important to convey when handing over a patient. In trauma meetings, learn how radiographs are best described in terms of the bone involved, fracture type, closed or open nature, any displacement or angulation and the presence or absence of associated neurovascular complications. Notice how there are often several approaches to managing the same case depending on the experience and background of the lead clinician.

> This is a rare opportunity to be in a room with so many senior clinicians. Observe how the cases are presented and which key points of the imaging are mentioned.

Clerking

One of the greatest learning tools is to take a focused history, examine the patient and then think of the differential diagnoses and management plan. This very active process draws together your detailed knowledge of a condition and forces you to think widely to consider differentials. It also allows you to practise the relevant examination and then to present the case to a senior doctor. Each stage of the above is extremely useful, and is excellent practice for OSCEs, where you will have to present your findings to an examiner. By the time a patient reaches a general ward they may have been clerked three or four times and will have learnt to tell their history in a medicalized, 'textbook' fashion. Initial signs such as wheeze in asthma, chronic obstructive pulmonary disease (COPD), bibasal crepitations of cardiac failure or hyper-resonant percussion note of a pneumothorax may have been treated and no longer present. Consequently the best places to practise taking a searching history and picking up classic signs are early on in a patient's stay – typically the acute medical unit, the emergency department and surgical admissions unit.

> Clerking a patient is one of the most well-rounded learning experiences, which uses many simultaneous input modalities (refer to Chapter 3 for theories on different input modalities).

This is a great opportunity to practise your systems enquiry. This list of screening questions for each body system should be written down, uploaded to your memory banks, and appear as a slick stream of concise questions that accurately and rapidly screens the cardiac, respiratory, gastrointestinal, neurological and rheumatological systems.

You don't have the time to perform a full examination of every system (and neither do you need to), but you should take the opportunity to do a careful and full examination of the relevant system following your history. The other systems should be treated to a rapid examination in a screening fashion.

It will be rare that in such a setting you will find a doctor to watch you examine, so ideally be watched by a fellow student. If there isn't anybody to do this, don't worry: your examination findings will be carefully dissected when you present, and it will become clear if there is any relevant part of the examination routine you have omitted.

PITFALLS

Don't just randomly choose a patient and start assessing them.

- Often the team can advise specific patients who may have a typical history, for example colicky right upper quadrant pain and vomiting in a patient with biliary colic, or classic signs such as dull percussion note, bronchial breathing and increased vocal resonance in a patient with lobar pneumonia.

- In areas such as the emergency department there is a pressure on doctors to see patients rapidly, so make sure the team is happy for you to see a particular patient. In practice this is often the third or fourth patient to be seen in time order, and results in less pressure upon you.

- Start by explaining to the patient that you are a student doctor, and gain consent. When you are finished taking a history and examining the patient, thank them, let them know that you are going to present their case to a senior doctor, and *never* answer any questions regarding waiting times, treatment options or potentially worrying diagnoses.

I definitely learnt more about managing acute presentations of medical and surgical conditions through clerking and presenting patients than from any book or teaching session.

RB, Oxford medical graduate

Clinics

There is significant learning potential to be found in many clinics as they have a high concentration of patients with advanced clinical signs. Many of these patients are suffering from chronic diseases which are stable and managed on an outpatient basis, and therefore highly likely to feature in your final exams.

One word of caution is that a major factor to take into account is the clinician you are sitting in with, who is not necessarily the consultant in charge. Talk to colleagues who have recently completed that attachment to find out which clinics are best not only for signs, but also in terms of the willingness of the registrar or consultant to teach and allow you to examine patients. Sometimes a particular clinic may always be extremely busy and understaffed, leading to a high state of tension, which is not student friendly and you may feel like you are slowing things down and just getting in everybody's way.

> I found clinics were hugely variable, ranging from exceptionally helpful clinicians showing you hundreds of signs to cold, unfriendly clinics where I was told to sit in the corner and then ignored.
>
> MP, recent Imperial graduate

A few clinics to consider making time for:

- **General medical clinics**. An excellent source of advanced clinical signs. Unusual signs to make a special effort to view will vary according to the type of clinic:

  - Cardiology: preoperative assessment clinic to examine in particular the common murmurs of AS, MR and AR, which have the highest likelihood of appearing in your exams.
  - Respiratory: pulmonary fibrosis, lobectomy/pneumonectomy scars, lung transplant, Horner's syndrome, intrinsic muscle wasting of the hands (Pancoast's syndrome) and severe COPD.
  - Gastroenterology: advanced signs of chronic liver disease, including significant ascites, extra-intestinal manifestations of inflammatory bowel disease.
  - Endocrinology: classic clinical features of acromegaly, Addison's disease, Cushing's syndrome, thyroid disease and diabetic complications including Charcot joints.
  - Diabetic eye clinic: if you get a fundoscopy station in your OSCE, you will be expected to perform a slick and competent examination, which is difficult as it is an infrequently performed examination and you may not recognize the different stages of diabetic retinopathy. The odds are that in a fundoscopy station the changes are those of diabetic retinopathy with the possibility of photocoagulation therapy signs. Take maximum advantage of these patients who have had their pupils dilated and perform a careful examination using a handheld ophthalmoscope. See the ophthalmology section in Chapter 2 for further details. Gain confidence at rapidly assessing the red reflex, fundus and four quadrants of each eye.

> I would definitely encourage every student to attend a diabetic eye clinic in the months leading up to finals. I was able to polish my fundoscopy examination and see a huge spectrum of diabetic eye complications.
>
> IL, graduate from Manchester medical school

- **Neurology clinic**. This is a great opportunity to hone your cranial and peripheral nerve examination while under the watchful eye of an experienced neurologist. Balanced against this is a word of caution against incorporating every single constructive criticism into your examination, as you will end up with an esoteric collection of quirky and quite specialist examination techniques. Don't forget that your ultimate aim is to produce a slick, orthodox examination which almost all examiners would be happy to see. It may not be a neurologist examining you and they may not understand or see the point of an unusual examination technique. Conditions to look out for include:

  - Peripheral neuropathies, eg Median, ulnar or radial nerve lesions;
  - Multiple sclerosis;
  - Motor neurone disease;
  - Charcot–Marie–Tooth syndrome;
  - Patients referred for headache, seizures or dizziness, as this could appear as a history station in your OSCE exam.

- **Rheumatology clinic**. Most of the conditions are stable and treated on an outpatient basis, so this is a rare opportunity to see classic signs of fairly advanced stages of disease. Try to examine the major conditions including:

  - Rheumatoid arthritis;
  - Osteoarthritis;
  - Gout and pseudogout;
  - Psoriatic arthritis;
  - Ankylosing spondylitis;
  - SLE;
  - Systemic sclerosis.

Pay particular attention to any extra-articular manifestations such as pulmonary fibrosis, cardiac murmurs, eye disease and skin changes. Practise your joint examinations before attending, especially the examination of the hands, shoulders, hips and knees. It is a fantastic opportunity to be able to examine these patients with classic signs, and you will maximize your uptake if you are able to perform a good joint examination.

For surgical clinics, refer to the surgery section in Chapter 2, 'The specialties'.

Don't forget that the majority of patients to be found in a finals examination have to be well enough to sit and be examined for an entire day, and so will generally have stable, chronic conditions which are principally managed on an outpatient basis – in clinic!

Theatres

A common misconception is that the best way to learn about surgery is by attending theatre. Unfortunately, most theatre time as a student will be spent either standing scrubbed but falling asleep holding a retractor, or simply standing too far away to see what is going on.

We aren't saying that theatre is a waste of time, just that if you don't have adequate preparation, clear learning objectives and, importantly, clear 'withdrawal' criteria, then you will almost certainly conclude a four-hour afternoon in theatres with a sore arm, tired legs from standing in one spot, and a zero per cent increase in your knowledge of surgery for finals. This last part is important, as for the budding surgeons there is a wealth of peripheral knowledge to be gained by learning different surgical techniques and approaches, and talking to the surgeon. The same cannot be said for the majority of students, whose aim is to learn some useful surgery for finals and perhaps have an enjoyable and interesting few hours.

One suggested approach which has a high likelihood of resulting in a productive time in theatre is outlined below.

Preparation

- Find out which cases are on the list for that session (am or pm). Ideally these cases represent common conditions (see Chapter 2, 'The specialties'), which have a reasonable likelihood of appearing in your surgical finals.

- Try to find out which members of the team will be in theatre; if there are too many people you will get forgotten, and if there is only one surgeon they may not have the time to teach. Ideally there are two senior surgeons present, one who can concentrate on operating and one who can take the time to go through things with you.

- Read up on the conditions, surgical approach, relevant anatomy and common postoperative complications.

- Define your learning objectives – for example, do you want to consolidate the anatomy of the area in question, understand first hand the surgical approach or ask the surgeon about the most commonly encountered complications?

- Try to clerk the patient beforehand to take a brief history and perform an examination of the relevant system.

I definitely found the team more willing to engage and teach me once they realized that I had clerked the patient and read about the operation.

TH, Bristol medical graduate

Try to consider the situation from the surgeon's point of view. They will be a lot more willing to teach you if you have shown some effort in terms of clerking the patient, reading up on the subject and getting scrubbed up.

Theatre

- Get there early, ie *never* get there late or you will irritate the surgeon and there is then even less reason to lose focus from operating and teach you.

- *Learn how to scrub up* – scrub nurses or junior members of the team are probably best to ask.

- Stand to the side once scrubbed up and then approach the operating table only when invited to do so by the surgeon.

- If you aren't scrubbing up, then try to stand somewhere *out of the way* but where you can both communicate with the surgeon and hopefully see some parts of the operation (use a footstool to gain the required height if necessary).

- Take a surgical book in with you as there will inevitably be moments when you are between patients or aren't scrubbed in, when you can at least read up on some surgical topics.

Always be aware of the uncanny ability of a medical student to stand in the wrong place at the wrong time...be aware of who and what is around you at all times.

Dialogue

- If the surgical team aren't forthcoming with questions or information, take the initiative and try asking some questions. If you are getting terse replies, back off and try again later. If you have no luck, then think about withdrawing (see withdrawal criteria, below).

- Keep questions concise and to the point as the surgeon has to concentrate for the operation and is doing you a favour by taking the occasional moment out to teach you.

Withdrawal criteria

- Time-honoured lines such as 'teaching' or 'supervisions' are still accepted, and you should consider them if:
  - despite your best efforts, the team is ignoring you;
  - you aren't learning anything;
  - there are several back-to-back operations of the same type, eg three hernia repairs.

- Action: thank the surgeon for their time, be prepared to answer the 'Tell me three things you have learnt today' question, and leave discreetly.

> If you are not learning anything, then you are probably wasting your time; consider changing location early once you realize you are not in a good learning environment.

Library

This is a great resource and grossly underused by most students. At its most basic level it functions as a comfortable environment to study. Meeting rooms can sometimes be booked for small groups to discuss a topic or carry out a question-and-answer session on a recent lecture. It will usually hold multiple copies of core textbooks for all specialties. This is a fantastic opportunity to try out different books before you invest in any of them (see Chapter 14, 'Book reviews', for reviews of commonly used core textbooks).

Electronic resources are growing in both their breadth and depth, and include:

- E-learning modules;
- Videos on examination technique;
- Multiple-choice questions from past papers;
- Lecture slides and videos;
- Course outline, curriculum and structure;
- Access to journals;
- Electronic portfolios;
- Forums for open discussion about your course and commonly encountered problems.

Librarians are experts at literature searching and can give valued assistance when researching an essay topic. Remember to seek their help early when undertaking a more detailed piece of work such as an end-of-attachment essay or dissertation.

> Don't be afraid of the library. Invest time early on to find out the range of resources available so you can build them into your revision plan.

Summary

- There are many areas of the hospital which offer high returns to the smart student, and it is important to make time for each of them.

- Set yourself realistic goals before each learning opportunity, and let the clinician know what they are. This allows both of you to focus on key areas and increase the likelihood of a productive session.

- Effort from you to help out on ward rounds and with ward jobs should be matched by teaching from the team.

- Work as a team with fellow students to compile a list of interesting clinical cases.

- When attending meetings, learn how to present a case concisely and take note of the different management strategies used by different clinicians.

- Make time to regularly clerk patients with common presentations such as shortness of breath, chest pain, abdominal pain and headache.

- Clinics offer a high throughput of patients with florid signs.

- Never just turn up for theatre without adequate preparation and defined learning objectives.

CHAPTER 2

The specialties

Modern medical training is extraordinarily diverse, and covers over 30 different specialties including radiology, public health, ethics and law, general practice, and anaesthetics.

Five of these are usually covered in greater detail and over a longer period: paediatrics, surgery, pathology, obstetrics and gynaecology, and psychiatry; these often have their own exams, and we will try to guide you through the key skills in each specialty and outline a strategy to gain the most from what is often a limited amount of time allocated to each.

We also cover dermatology and ophthalmology, which are given only a brief time in the medical school course, yet examiners expect a strong working knowledge of a narrow set of conditions.

Paediatrics

● Clinical examination

● Core topics

● Notes on OSCE examinations

This is definitely a specialty not to be crammed or taken lightly. Most medical schools have deemed this a critical specialty and the end-of-attachment exams often reflect this, with students failing this having to retake the attachment or even the entire year.

Medical schools often draw up fairly comprehensive schedules to ensure you get wide-ranging experience in paediatrics, which, while interesting, is probably not finals focused. In your first week, aim to get a copy of past papers and start to understand which core topics in each system the examiners would like you to have a good knowledge of. Talk to foundation doctors who took your exam in previous years to get a feel of which cases are commonly examined in OSCEs.

There is a lot to cover in a relatively short time, so be finals focused from day one.

Clinical examination

Take every available opportunity to perform an examination of a child. It is fairly common to go through several days of lectures, clinics, meetings and ward rounds and not actually formally examine a child all week. You should differentiate between the paediatric and neonatal examinations; build a different examination routine for each.

A common reason for inadequate practice in examining children is simply the fear of a screaming, irritable child, and the fact that they may not be old enough to obey commands and be cooperative during an examination. Inability to alter your voice and approach in order to gain rapid rapport with a child will be noted by your examiners, who will rightly assume that you haven't taken the time to examine enough children.

Flexibility is key; you must be able to perform your examination in short stages which may be completely out of order to the orthodox routine with the adult. For example, it is entirely reasonable to auscultate the heart and lungs at an early stage while the child is settled and cooperative, as murmurs will be challenging in an upset, crying, tachycardic child. Take every available opportunity to smile and talk to the parents in a friendly manner; if they are comfortable with you and seem to like you, then the child will note this and be a little happier for you to examine them.

Make a conscious effort to examine children of any age, from neonates to teenagers. Learn how to tailor the examination to fit the age of the child.

There are many areas of the paediatric examination which differ from that of an adult. Below is a guide to clinical examination which focuses on these key areas. Note that it does not represent a detailed and full examination – for this we would refer you to a paediatric textbook (see Chapter 14, 'Book reviews').

- General inspection:
    - Well or unwell: often resulting from a subconscious process where you scan the patient from top to toe, taking one to two seconds;
    - Nutritional status: obese or underweight;
    - Dysmorphism: think of common syndromes, and hence the collection of physical signs you should expect with them, eg Down's, Hurler, Edwards, Turner and Patau;
    - Colour: pallor, jaundice or cyanosis;
    - Hydration status: skin turgor and mucous membranes;
    - Clubbing: most likely to be due to cystic fibrosis or cyanotic congenital heart disease.

> A lot of the examination findings will be made on inspection, and you should allow more time than you would when examining an adult to carry out 'end of the bed' inspection, which includes time spent talking to the parents during which you can observe the child.

- Respiratory:
    - Added airway noises such as stridor or wheeze;
    - Supplemental oxygen use;
    - Respiratory rate: you need to have an idea of normal values relating to age;
    - Work of breathing: you should be able to describe the presence or absence of increased work of breathing as shown by the use of accessory muscles, subcostal and intercostal recession, and tracheal tug;
    - Chest wall deformity: pectus carinatum or excavatum.
- Cardiovascular:
    - Cyanosis: best seen on the tongue and lips. Most commonly seen in association with cyanotic congenital heart disease such as Tetralogy of Fallot (decreased pulmonary blood flow) or transposition of the great arteries (abnormal mixing);

- Operative scars such as midline sternotomy or left lateral thoracotomy;
- Signs of heart failure: failure to thrive, sweating, tachypnoeic, tachycardic, gallop rhythm, cardiomegaly and hepatomegaly;
- Femoral pulses: abnormal in coarctation of the aorta, where they may be faint or not palpable in infants, and delayed in older children.

- Abdominal:
  - Jaundice: causes are best categorized by age of onset;
  - Hepatomegaly: think of primary liver disease such as hepatitis and polycystic disease, malignancy such as leukaemia and Wilms' tumour, and storage disorders;
  - Splenomegaly: think of malignancy such as leukaemia and lymphoma, infections such as malaria and leishmaniasis, and haemolytic anaemias;
  - Genital examination: this should be routine in infants and young children, but only if specifically indicated in older children;
  - Digital rectal examination: unlike an adult examination, this is not performed routinely. Even if performed in the context of specific presentations such as the acute abdomen, most clinicians would argue that the results are difficult to interpret and do not alter management.

- Neurological:
  - Inspection: unlike the adult examination, much of the paediatric examination is based on careful observation of behaviour at rest, while playing with toys, and the child's interaction with other children and adults;
  - Important activities to observe include:
    — Movement: standing from lying supine (look for Gowers' sign), pattern of walking and running, general posture when at rest;
    — Playing: look for interaction with other children, coordination and ability to grasp and transfer objects;
    — Drawing or writing: if able to perform either, this is an excellent test of coordination, grasp, vision and neurodevelopmental stage.
  - If the child is able to follow basic commands and you have built a good rapport, you may be able to assess aspects of the cranial and peripheral nerve examination by making it into a game. The examiners will understand if despite your best efforts you are unable to perform anything more than a gross, mostly observational neurological examination.
  - Neurodevelopmental stage: it is vital that you get used to rapidly estimating a child's developmental age through assessment of their 'milestones', which

are commonly divided into language, motor, social/emotional, coordination and visual. There are many different types of developmental charts which all vary slightly, so stick to an established source or text.

● Eyes, ENT and lymph nodes:

– You should incorporate ophthalmoscopy into your examination as an absent red reflex is seen in cataracts and retinoblastoma.

– The examiners will often stop you as you go to perform the ENT examination, as parents do not want their child subjected to numerous unpleasant tongue depressors and otoscope examinations.

As with all extended examination skills, even if on most occasions you expect the examiner to stop you as you go to perform, for example, otoscopy or test the corneal reflex or jaw jerk, you should nevertheless be prepared to carry out or describe fully this part of the examination.

● Things to ask for at the end: weight and growth charts or 'red book', urine dipstick, pulse oximetry and temperature chart.

● Neonatal examination; vital aspects:

– Ask for gestational age and birthweight.

– Fully undress the baby.

– Use a top-down approach, starting with the fontanelles.

– Comment on pallor and jaundice.

– Look for a red reflex (to exclude cataracts).

– Check for cleft palate.

– Listen to the heart sounds and lungs before the baby starts crying.

– Palpate the femoral pulses.

– Pick the baby up to assess tone.

– Check the back and spine, looking for signs of spina bifida.

– Perform the Barlow and Ortolani tests for developmental dysplasia of the hips.

I found there was a massive mental hurdle to examining infants and young children, and that my examination was initially very hesitant. After persevering and examining as many children as I could, my confidence grew and my examination became a lot more slick and assured.

SP, recent UCL graduate

Core topics

The potential list of conditions which are commonly examined is much smaller than you might have feared. Topics to focus on are those commonly encountered in clinical practice and include:

- Respiratory:
  - Asthma. Typical symptom type and pattern, common precipitants, effects on school and play, sleep disturbance, exacerbation frequency and current treatment regime. Both acute and chronic management (look up the BTS guidelines), the difficulty of peak flow testing in children, different inhaler devices which are used for different age groups. Importance of regular outpatient follow-up to review symptom control, use of rescue inhaler, medication compliance and side effects.
  - Bronchiolitis. Typical disease progression and clinical features, indications for admission which include saturations of below 95% on air, less than 50% of normal feed volume in a 24-hour period, apnoeic episodes and signs of dehydration.
  - Croup. Typical clinical features, treatment options depending on severity as measured by a clinical score such as the Westley croup score, and indications for admission. Life-threatening differentials such as epiglottitis, bacterial tracheitis and foreign body obstruction of the upper airway.
  - Cystic fibrosis. Genetic basis and pathophysiology, screening, clinical features divided both temporally and into systems affected. This is an excellent example of multidisciplinary team management of a chronic disease.
- Gastrointestinal:
  - Vomiting; medical and surgical causes.
  - Diarrhoea. Be able to clinically assess the degree of dehydration in terms of mild (<5%), moderate (5–10%), severe (>10%), and understand the different approaches to treatment with respect to oral rehydration and intravenous rehydration. Learn to calculate fluid requirements and understand the dangers of over-rapid correction of hyponatraemia.
  - Pyloric stenosis. Typical age and features at presentation, value of a test feed, classic hypochloraemic alkalosis and hypokalaemic biochemical disturbance. Ultrasound diagnosis and pyloromyotomy.

- Acute abdominal pain:
    - Surgical causes: appendicitis, obstruction, intussusception, inguinal hernia and Meckel's diverticulitis;
    - Medical causes: gastroenteritis, UTI, DKA, Henoch-Schönlein purpura and constipation;
    - Other: testicular torsion, basal pneumonia.

- Nutrition:
    - Differentials of short stature. Congenital adrenal hyperplasia as a cause of abnormal sexual differentiation.
    - Feeding. Differentials of failure to thrive, rickets, comparison of breast and formula feeding.

- Endocrine:
    - Diabetes mellitus. Pathophysiology, spectrum of presentation, including the management of DKA and hypoglycaemia. Diagnostic tests, different insulin regimes, importance of patient compliance with dietary measures and blood glucose monitoring. Long-term complications including neurological, micro and macrovascular, focusing on the eyes, kidneys, heart, skin and feet.
    - Cushing's syndrome. Common causes and clinical features.
    - Inborn errors of metabolism. Presenting features in the neonatal period. Disorders of aminoacid and carbohydrate metabolism, and organic acidaemias in terms of brief clinical features and treatment.

- Neurology:
    - Epilepsy. Main types and secondary causes of seizures including meningoencephalitis, head injury and electrolyte disturbance. Algorithm for the management of status epilepticus. Common side effects of frequently prescribed anticonvulsants (role in patient compliance).
    - Febrile convulsions. Typical age range, clinical picture, prognosis, typical management of a first and subsequent episode depending on age and the identification of a source of fever.
    - Cerebral palsy. Causes (antenatal, intrapartum and postnatal), presentation and multidisciplinary nature of long-term management.
    - Duchenne's and Becker's muscular dystrophies. Presenting features, diagnostic investigations and key differences.

- Cardiology:
    - Cyanotic and non-cyanotic congenital heart disease. Examples of the most common causes of each type and the major circulatory changes from birth.

- Heart failure. Classic features in the history such as poor feeding and failure to thrive, breathlessness on feeding or minimal exertion and episodes of sweating. Signs (see above in examination section), common causes in neonates and infants.
- SVT. Use of vagal manoeuvres, intravenous adenosine and synchronized DC cardioversion.

● Haematology/oncology:
  - ITP. Typical history, presentation and progression. Indications for corticosteroids, immunoglobulin infusion and splenectomy.
  - HSP. Classic pentad, pathophysiology, indications for corticosteroids, long-term renal complications.
  - Leukaemias:
    — Classic presentation as a result of local effects such as a mass or pressure effects, secondary effects such as long bone pain, or general symptoms such as anorexia, lethargy and loss of weight.
    — Acute lymphoblastic leukaemia. Frequency, presentation, chemotherapy, prognosis.
  - Lymphomas:
    — Hodgkin's and non-Hodgkin's types. Main similarities and differences with respect to pathology, presentation, typically affected age group, treatment and prognosis.
  - Brain tumours. Most common types, typical presenting features and long-term growth, endocrine and neuropsychological complications.
  - Neuroblastoma and Wilms' tumour. Differentials of an abdominal mass, diagnostic investigations, treatment options and prognosis.

● Infectious disease:
  - The approach to the investigation and management of the febrile child.
  - Common childhood infections. Measles, mumps, rubella, varicella, herpes and parvovirus in terms of typical incubation period, special clinical features and particular complications.
  - Staphylococcus and streptococcus with respect to cellulitis, necrotizing fasciitis and toxic shock syndrome.
  - Kawasaki's disease. Typical case history often consisting of prolonged fever with conjunctivitis, erythematous mucous membranes, cervical lymphadenopathy and then a rash and peeling skin of the hands and feet. Pathophysiology, life-threatening complications and first-line treatment.

- Meningitis. Varied presentation and common organisms according to age group, immediate treatment, long-term complications.
- Urinary tract infections. Investigation pathway after a first UTI which aims to identify vesicoureteric reflux, renal scars and major structural abnormalities. Other key factors include an atypical organism or recurrent infections, both of which lead to more urgent and thorough investigation. Common complications and treatment.
- Standard immunization schedule.

● Social/environmental:
  - Non-accidental injury; 'red flags' at presentation to emergency services such as:
    — Delay in reporting, history not consistent with the injury, history inconsistent between caregivers, injury inconsistent with developmental age, recurrent injury patterns, and unusual reactions from parents;
    — Unusual injury types such as rib fractures, bruising on the back or buttocks, burns, including flexures or without splash marks.

● Genetics:
  - Syndromes to know well include Down's, Klinefelter's and Turners.
    — Genetic defect, major clinical features, complications.
  - Syndromes to know in brief include Edwards, Patau, Noonan's, Williams', Prader-Willi and Hurler.
    — Phenotypic features, three to five main clinical features.
  - Examples of autosomal dominant, autosomal recessive and X-linked recessive conditions;
  - Difficulties associated with genetic counselling.

● Perinatal medicine; screening tests used both non-invasive (ultrasound) and invasive (amniocentesis, chorionic villus sampling, foetal blood or tissue sampling);

● Neonatal medicine; differentials for jaundice.

The management of any chronic paediatric condition is invariably multidisciplinary in nature and reflects the complex nature of disease. Answers regarding the management of conditions such as asthma, diabetes and epilepsy should therefore state early on that you recognize the multidisciplinary approach. Key people to mention are the paediatric consultant who leads the team, the GP who coordinates the team, the parents who will be the main carers at home, the nurse specialist who provides a community link, the physiotherapist, occupational therapist, dietician, psychologist, health visitor, teachers and school nurse.

Notes on OSCE examinations

As you prepare for your paediatric finals, be they OSCE or long case, make sure you know exactly which format the exam takes. Questions you should be able to answer are:

- Does the OSCE examination have a standard format where there is a station on each and every system?

- Does the timing differ, with more time allowed per examination compared to the standard finals OSCE? Get used to performing the relevant examination within the time frame.

- Is there a neonatal station using a mannequin?

- How many history-taking and other communication skills stations are there?

- Is it possible that I could be shown a paediatric chest radiograph, limb radiograph or ECG?

- Can I check a child's peak flow and inhaler technique?

- Can I plot a child's weight on the appropriate growth chart?

> Do not assume that the format of the paediatric OSCE follows that of your general medicine/surgery exams.

Surgery

- Things to go to once or twice

- Complications; both general and operation specific

- Differentials for the acute abdomen

- Clinical summaries of appendicitis, acute pancreatitis, biliary colic/cholecystitis, ischaemic bowel, ruptured AAA and bowel obstruction

- Important anatomy

The approach to preparation for surgical finals differs from medical finals. The format of the final exam and type of questions asked are often very different from medical OSCE stations. Questions are often more straightforward, following a standard format and revolving around the causes, types and treatment of different conditions and the nature and complications of different surgical procedures.

Surgical conditions are often well suited to short examinations, often requiring little more than good observation skills and the ability to describe what you are seeing concisely, using the correct terms.

Terminology is extremely important in surgery. Use of incorrect descriptors such as fistula and abscess are likely to upset the examiners.

Knowledge of different abdominal scar sites is vital. Be able to make an educated guess as to the nature of the possible operation when shown a scar anywhere on the abdomen; think of which organs and areas a particular incision allows access to. Take the time to go to transplant wards, general surgical wards, clinics and gastro-intestinal medical wards to familiarize yourself with more unusual but important scars such as nephrectomy, 'rooftop' and 'Mercedes Benz' types.

Things to go to once or twice

- Preoperative clinics. Help the team out with preoperative clerking, thereby learning the importance of screening and checking the general health of patients for surgery. Some of the main learning points are:

  - Operations often involve expected and unexpected haemorrhage. Preparation therefore requires the blood bank to have blood 'grouped and saved' for those operations in which little blood loss is anticipated, for example a laparoscopic cholecystectomy or appendicectomy. In emergency operations or those in which large blood losses are anticipated the blood bank should be notified and blood cross-matched. Have an idea about typical units required for an abdominal aortic aneurysm and an elective hemicolectomy.

  - Written consent should be taken by an appropriate team member who is familiar with the operation and is able to offer details regarding the procedure and complications.

  - Diabetic patients are often placed first on the list, and require a sliding-scale regime of intravenous insulin intraoperatively.

  - Patients who are MRSA, HepB or C or HIV positive are placed at the end of a list as the theatre has to be specially cleaned afterwards.

  - Chest radiographs required if pre-existing cardiorespiratory disease or older than 65 years old.

I found preoperative clinics fantastic for examining femoral and inguinal hernias.

MT, foundation 2 doctor, John Radcliffe Hospital

- Colonoscopy. This is an extremely important investigation which is very commonly performed, and therefore it is expected that you understand the procedure in detail including indications, complications and alternatives.
  - Differentiate between a rigid and flexible sigmoidoscopy, colonoscopy and 'virtual' colonoscopy performed either with endoscopic capsules or with CT.
  - Understand where the majority of colorectal cancers are distributed and therefore why a flexible sigmoidoscopy is often a reasonable first-choice investigation rather than every patient undergoing a colonoscopy.
  - Common complications include haemorrhage, perforation, infection and problems related to the sedation or anaesthetic.

- General surgical clinics:
  - One of the few places with a high number of preoperative hernias.
  - Observe and be guided through the huge range of abdominal scars and which operations are commonly performed through them.
  - Make a note of common postoperative complications in terms of their severity, frequency and time frame.

- Vascular clinic:
  - Practise your vascular examination, paying particular attention to the differences between arterial and venous disease and the typical spectrum of skin changes seen with each.
  - Look at some magnetic resonance angiograpy (MRA) images and get an understanding of commonly performed endovascular procedures and operations.

- For any operation you should be clear in your mind about the following points:
  - Indications;
  - An outline of the main steps of the operation itself;
  - Complications divided either into major/minor or early/late;
  - Postoperative care and follow-up.

There are certain operations which are more commonly asked about in finals and as such you should learn them in greater detail and ensure that you follow at least one case of each to theatre:

- Laparoscopic appendicectomy;

- Laparoscopic cholecystectomy;

- Inguinal hernia repair;

- Mastectomy;

- Bowel resection and stoma formation.

Postoperative complications

Postoperative complications are a major problem and source of prolonged hospital stays, so examiners can rightly expect a detailed working knowledge. One way to divide this up is into general complications and those which are operation specific.

Some complications can be seen with any operation, and are termed 'general' postoperative complications:

- **Infection**. Pneumonia, urinary tract infection and cellulitis are common in any patient who has had a general anaesthetic, possibly a catheter, a midline laparotomy scar, and had to lie supine for a week due to pain.

- **Hypotension**. Possibly due to haemorrhage, but also more 'medical' causes such as myocardial infarction and sepsis.

- **DVT and pulmonary embolus**. Especially in operations which limit the mobility of a patient afterwards; examples include laparotomies, major pelvic surgery or lower limb orthopaedic surgery.

- **Pain**. Significant and uncontrolled pain after an operation can be difficult to control and results in a very negative patient experience. Options for postoperative analgesia include 'standard' control which revolves around the analgesic ladder with opioid drugs at the highest level. Be aware of advanced techniques which include patient-controlled analgesia (PCA) and epidurals.

- **Decreased urine output**. The most common cause is pre-renal, ie insufficient fluids given intravenously. Renal causes are generally due to acute tubular necrosis from the antibiotics administered, transfusion of blood products, or SIRS.

Learn the operation-specific complications, including a rough idea of their frequency for common operations involving areas such as:

- Small bowel: short gut syndrome, malabsorption and dumping syndrome.

- Large bowel: postoperative ileus is very common. Fistulae can form or anastomoses may leak.

- Laparotomy: wound dehiscence, especially in the elderly who may be malnourished or suffer from malignancy.

- Gallbladder and biliary tree (laparoscopic): conversion to open procedure (1–5%), bile duct injury, retained stones, strictures and pancreatitis.

- Thyroid: recurrent laryngeal nerve palsy occurs in approximately 1% and can be permanent, leading to hoarseness. Hypoparathyroidism leading to hypocalcaemia occurs in approximately 2%.

- Breast: lymphoedema of the ipsilateral arm in up to 20% of those having axillary node sampling or dissection.

> Be able to talk about the general and specific complications for any operation, breaking them down temporally, for example into early and late.

Differentials for the acute abdomen

Examiners would like you to know the differentials for the acute abdomen, broken down by quadrant and then further divided by system. For example, the differentials of right lower quadrant pain are:

- Gastrointestinal: appendicitis, strangulated hernia, Meckel's diverticulitis, Crohn's disease, perforated caecum;

- Gynaecological: ruptured ectopic pregnancy, salpingitis, ovarian torsion or haemorrhage into an ovarian cyst;

- Urological: ureteric calculus, pyelonephritis.

You should be able to generate a list organized in the same manner for each quadrant of the abdomen. Remember that 'common things are common' and that you should provide two or three of the most likely differentials first, and then list the other causes by system (see Chapter 9, 'Active answering').

First-line investigations are chosen as they are rapidly able to aid the confirmation or exclusion of life-threatening causes of abdominal pain. They include:

- Amylase – acute pancreatitis, with lesser rises in local perforation and inflammation such as severe gastritis and cholecystitis.

- Liver function tests and inflammatory markers – acute cholecystitis, ascending cholangitis.

- Urea and electrolytes – renal dysfunction associated with a renal calculus, acute renal failure as a marker of systemic upset and therefore disease severity in pancreatitis.

- Erect chest radiograph – bowel perforation produces free air which is visible on the erect film. Important to rule out basal pneumonia as a differential in a vague historian with atypical signs.

- Supine abdominal radiograph – dilated small or large bowel loops in obstruction, a 'coffee bean' sign of sigmoid volvulus, and toxic megacolon as a surgical complication of inflammatory bowel disease.

- Urine dipstick – haematuria seen in approximately 80% patients with renal calculi, leukocytes often seen in local inflammation such as appendicitis. Helpful to rule out a urinary tract infection as a cause of generalize lower abdominal pain.

- Urine βHCG – ruptured ectopic pregnancy.

- Arterial blood gas – lactic acidosis seen classically in mesenteric ischaemia or infarction, and in shock resulting from a leaking abdominal aortic aneurysm.

Clinical summaries

Particular conditions to learn in detail are covered below.

Appendicitis. Wide spectrum of clinical presentations depending on age and location of the appendix. Atypical presentations such as 'gastroenteritis' especially in the paediatric patient. Helpful clinical features such as Rovsing's sign and tests for local peritonism such as guarding and percussion tenderness. Lack of a sufficiently specific and rapid bedside test hence scoring systems such as the Alvarado score have been developed, but this lacks sensitivity even when combined with ultrasound scanning. Increasing use of ultrasound and CT to guide management but the gold standard remains operation and direct visualization.

Acute pancreatitis. The two most common causes are gallstones and alcohol, but other causes are covered by the mnemonic GET SMASHED (trauma, steroids, mumps, autoimmune scorpion venom, hypothermia/hyperlipidaemia/hypercalcaemia, ERCP and drugs). It is vital to identify those patients who have severe disease so that they can have more invasive monitoring and treatment of complications such as ARDS, DIC, renal failure and shock. The Modified Glasgow criteria or Ranson's criteria are used to identify severe cases and incorporate factors such as paO2, age, neutrophil count, renal function and AST levels. Late complications include pseudocyst formation, abscesses and pancreatic necrosis.

Biliary colic and cholecystitis. These two conditions are part of a spectrum of disease caused by gallstones. Biliary colic is managed on an outpatient basis with good analgesia, ultrasound to visualize stones and an elective laparoscopic cholecystectomy. Indications for inpatient management include stone impaction in the cystic duct causing local inflammation, ie cholecystitis. Symptoms are often more severe, with right upper quadrant pain radiating to the right shoulder tip and accompanied by fever and vomiting. Murphy's sign is positive – inability to take a deep inspiration with the examining hand in the right subcostal region (due to impingement on the inflamed gallbladder) and absence of pain while performing the test on the left subcostal region. Management involves ruling out a perforation and admitting the patient for a cholecystectomy. Other complications requiring intervention include ascending cholangitis, which is where a gallstone lodges in the common bile duct, leading to proximal infection. Blockage of the pancreatic duct obstructs pancreatic drainage and can lead to acute pancreatitis.

Ischaemic bowel. Commonly missed due to the lack of clinical signs. Often the only clues are a patient who looks sick and who has abdominal pain but very little signs on examination, ie soft abdomen. They are often elderly vasculopaths who have arterial thrombosis or patients with chronic atrial fibrillation who throw off an embolus. They become shocked rapidly and blood gases show a lactic acidosis. Management involves fluid resuscitation, antibiotics and preparation for surgery to resect the segment of dead, typically small intestine.

AAA. One of the most important diagnoses to actively exclude in a middle-aged or elderly patient presenting with undifferentiated abdominal pain, especially if it is a 'first' presentation of pain suggestive of renal colic. Clues in the history include a constant or intermittent severe central pain radiating through to the back. On examination, signs include an expansile central mass and poor femoral pulses. Diagnosis can be rapidly achieved through ultrasound or CT, and once confirmed blood should be cross-matched for at least six units due to the potential for massive blood loss. Options for repair include endovascular and open surgical techniques.

Bowel obstruction. Key features on presentation include initial colicky abdominal pain, abdominal distension, constipation and vomiting. The picture progresses to more constant pain with or without peritonism if there is strangulation or perforation of bowel. An early supine abdominal radiograph helps to confirm the diagnosis and localize the site of obstruction. An erect chest radiograph allows you to identify free air resulting from perforation. Initial management is to insert a nasogastric tube, keep the patient nil by mouth and start intravenous fluids, commonly known as the 'drip and suck' regime. The need for surgery depends on whether the obstruction is complete or incomplete, the presence of strangulation, and whether it is large bowel obstruction with a competent ileo-caecal valve (closed loop obstruction leads to greater distension and chances of perforation).

Other core surgical topics include:

- Diverticulitis – common presentations and complications;
- Urology – renal calculi, carcinomas;
- Carcinoma – bowel, gastric, pancreatic.

> Examiners are surgical consultants who want to know that they can trust you to recognize a surgical emergency and institute the appropriate first-line management.

Important anatomy

It is rare in finals to be questioned at length regarding the detailed anatomy of a single area or of the anatomy of multiple areas of the body. However, you may well be asked to briefly describe the anatomy of some of the following areas which are deemed to have particular clinical significance:

- General surgery:
  - Inguinal canal;
  - Biliary tree;
  - Small and large intestines, with associated areas of vascular supply.
- Breast surgery:
  - Axillary lymphatic drainage.
- ENT:
  - Triangles of the neck;
  - Branches of the facial nerve.
- Vascular:
  - Venous drainage of the lower limb including saphenofemoral junction.
- Orthopaedics
  - Carpal and tarsal bones;
  - Rotator cuff muscles and ligaments of the shoulder;
  - Different types of femoral neck fractures;
  - Ligaments and menisci of the knee.

Pathology

● Learning resources and activities

● Core topics

Pathology is a unique subspecialty because its significance in medical school curricula varies immensely throughout the country; some medical schools have in-depth examinations on pathology as a separate topic, while other schools include it as part of medical finals. Certain schools can have specific lectures and teaching on the subject, and others leave it to be integrated into clinical education.

Given the variability of the requirements, it can be difficult to give an overview of pathology that will suit every student. We impress upon you the need to establish the level of pathology to be tested in your finals by talking to the assessment staff, peers and seniors, and tailor your revision to match this. It can vary from very little to entire papers!

Learning resources and opportunities

Many courses feature basic pathology in the early 'basic sciences' years, but it may be worth revisiting some elements of this in your revision for finals. Rather than going through entire sections and trying to commit them to memory, you may wish to include a small pathology section in your main revision notes, and therefore have access to key pathological concepts as part of your overall approach to finals.

Books play a critical role in revision and we have reviewed several popular pathology books in Chapter 14, giving an indication of which might be an appropriate level for medical students.

Attending post-mortems at hospitals is certainly an interesting way to gain first-hand visual experience of macroscopic pathology. There is another benefit to attending these sessions, in that you can discuss the macroscopic pathology with experts who consider this topic on a daily basis and relate it to clinical disease. If you prepare well for your post-mortem session, you can reinforce key points in your pathology by asking the pathologist to discuss certain topics; many students have found them to be excellent and willing teachers.

We stress that it is important to assess the amount of pathology that is expected from you in your final medical school year, and indeed in the examination itself. You may find that it will not be expressly tested in your medical finals. If this is the case, we remind you that understanding pathology is a vital part of being a capable and competent physician, and will aid in your diagnosis and management of patients. However, with specific regard to medical finals, try focusing on more clinical aspects which come up in exams.

Core topics

Pathology can be divided into basic and systemic pathology. Basic pathology describes the processes by which disease manifests. Systemic pathology describes how diseases of different systems occur.

Basic pathology is often less relevant than systemic pathology for your exams. However, there are some clinically relevant topics, including:

- Acute inflammatory processes and asthma;
- Inflammatory cytokines and anti-TNF therapy in autoimmune conditions;
- Cellular changes in stages of cancer, eg cervical cancer;
- Processes of atherosclerosis and risk factors in cardiovascular disease;
- Responses to viral and parasitic infections.

Systemic pathology topics:

- Cardiac:
  - Changes in myocardium over time following MI;
  - Mechanisms of post-MI complications including Dressler's syndrome, mural or papillary muscle rupture;
  - Endocarditis, primary and embolic effects, common pathogens;
  - Causes of each type of common heart valve disorders.
- Respiratory:
  - Types of bronchial carcinoma and their risk factors;
  - Endocrine secondary effects of carcinomas;
  - Mesothelioma;
  - Causes and effects of pulmonary embolism;
  - Lung infections including tuberculosis and abcesses;
  - Acute respiratory distress syndrome;
  - Mechanisms of COPD;
  - The role of the immune system in pneumoconiosis;
  - Genetics of cystic fibrosis, and mechanism;
  - Pulmonary hypertension; causes and effects.

- Gastrointestinal:
  - Balance of protective and destructive factors in peptic ulcer disease, and the adaptations of helicobacter pylori;
  - Oesophageal, gastric and small bowel tumours;
  - Large bowel tumours, staging, grading;
  - Crohn's disease and ulcerative colitis; characteristic macroscopic changes in the bowel for each disease.

- Renal:
  - Other causes of renal disease eg hypertension, diabetes;
  - Renal infection; pylenephritis, and its contrasting characteristics with UTI;
  - Inflammation of the kidneys, glomerulonephritis, interstitial nephritis;
  - Renal stone pathology;
  - Disruption to renal architecture in hydronephrosis.

- Hepatobiliary:
  - Mechanism and sequelae of acute and chronic pancreatitis;
  - Gallstone pathology;
  - Hepatitis including details of the liver viruses and their respective prognoses;
  - Hepatic cancer including hepatocellular carcinoma and metastatic liver CA;
  - Causes, cellular and architectural changes in cirrhosis;
  - Mechanism of alcoholic liver disease.

- Reproductive:
  - Prostatic cancer and its markers;
  - Testicular tumours and their subtypes;
  - Cervical carcinoma, its precursors, risk factors and immunization;
  - Fibroids;
  - Endometriosis investigation;
  - Orchitis.

- Neurological:
  - Stroke pathology, risk factors and the differences between haemorrhagic and ischaemic;
  - Brain infections; meningitis and brain abcesses;
  - Pathology of dementia including prion disease.

- Systemic disease:
  - A gross understanding of the pathology of amyloidosis and sarcoidosis;
  - HIV infection and its manifestation of AIDS;
  - Diabetes Mellitus and its complications.

Obstetrics and gynaecology

- The gynaecological history and examination;
- The obstetric history and examination;
- Navigating through the delivery suite.

This is often a very regimented attachment, with many compulsory clinics and practical skills to sign off.

The gynaecological history

This is an area that most male medical students will find particularly difficult initially, with unfamiliar terms and possibly embarrassing questions. Practise taking enough histories and this embarrassment will fade, and you will start to understand why the questions are vital in order to discriminate between the common acute presentations such as abdominal pain or vaginal bleeding.

Areas you need to ask about if the presenting complaint makes them relevant:

- **Menstrual history**. First day of last menstrual period (LMP), intermenstrual or postcoital bleeding, dysmenorrhoea, menorrhagia, cycle length/regularity.

- **Cervical smear history**. Last cervical smear and result, any previous abnormal results and what treatments were performed.

- **Sexual/contraceptive history**. If sexually active. is there superficial or deep dyspareunia? Contraceptive currently used and methods used previously, previous sexually transmitted infection.

- **Obstetric history**. Briefly ask about previous pregnancies in terms of when, type of delivery and any complications.

- **Past medical and surgical history**. Any major medical conditions, previous gynaecological operations, pelvic inflammatory disease, ectopic pregnancies.

- **Family history**. Breast or ovarian carcinoma.

The gynaecological examination

In your exam you may be required to perform a gynaecological examination on a mannequin. As part of your course you will probably need to be supervised/observed performing a specified number of speculum or bimanual examinations. It is valuable to practise on mannequins before approaching real patients, but remember to rehearse your 'patter' while examining the mannequins, which should include a request for a chaperone and private cubicle, ideally with a lockable door.

The obstetric history

- Age, gravidity (total number of times a woman has been pregnant), parity (total number of times a woman has given birth to a foetus older than 24 weeks gestation).

- Reason for current admission, for example abdominal pains, vaginal bleeding or routine check-up.

- Current pregnancy – first day of last menstrual period (LMP) and weeks of gestation, any complications so far in terms of bleeding, hypertension, or worsening of underlying medical conditions. Results of investigations such as ultrasound scans or prenatal tests performed so far.

- Previous complications of pregnancy:
    - Ectopic pregnancies;
    - Miscarriages;
    - Pre-eclampsia/eclampsia;
    - Diabetes.
- Gynaecological history. This should be brief and include assisted fertilization and gynaecological surgery.

- Social history. Smoking and alcohol history, support at home and occupation.

The obstetric examination

- This should be learnt from a good textbook and then further polished through observed practice.

- Try to make every effort to examine pregnant patients on the wards and in clinic so that you get used to using a gentle, understanding approach and estimating fetal lie and checking dates.

- Practise using a Pinard stethoscope to auscultate for a foetal heartbeat, but don't be disheartened if you struggle. Ultrasound dopplers are now widespread and are much more commonly used in practice.

> Your initial frustration at not being able to estimate foetal dates, lie and presentation will hopefully evaporate as you learn the subtleties of an accurate examination from experienced doctors and midwives.

Navigating through the delivery suite

The delivery suite is a veritable war zone, with student midwives competing to manage the delivery of a limited number of patients. There are definitely a few tips worth bearing in mind:

- The delivery suite is a fairly territorial area, with midwives trying to protect their own students and ensure them access to deliveries. The obstetric registrars will mostly be in theatre or clinic, so you will not have an advocate to secure you access to deliveries.

- Student midwives often gain consent of patients in the community, so there is no point wasting effort trying to gain consent from pre-consented patients.

- Midwives will often offer to consent a patient on your behalf. If at all possible ask to be introduced to the patient, but consent the patient yourself. By doing this you can dispel any preconceptions a patient may hold about medical students, and avoid any negative connotations which may be offered consciously or subconsciously by the midwife. Patients are generally very understanding about the needs of medical students and are unlikely to say no if asked in a polite and respectful way by a smiling but serious-looking medical student.

- There is a lot of waiting and being polite, respectful and knowing when to talk and when to fade into the background. Bring an O&G textbook and be prepared to sit quietly in the corner.

- Most medical schools have a specified minimum number of deliveries that each student must observe, and also deliver. While this sign-off sheet will be in the back of your mind, try to keep it from becoming the driving force for your visits to clinic or delivery suite. Acting in such a blinkered fashion will make you less receptive to opportunistic learning experiences such as discussing a case with an experienced midwife and learning from her past experiences, or following a patient who takes an unexpected trip to theatre for an emergency caesarean section.

- Nights are an excellent time for you to get hands-on experience with deliveries. Less competition between fellow students (medical and midwifery) allows you to 'float' between different expectant mothers (having gained a rapport and consent at the start of the night). This enables you to operate in a parallel fashion between different deliveries rather than in the serial fashion of a single patient, which occurs during day shifts. The resultant number of observed and participated deliveries can be as great as a factor of five compared to that of a day shift.

- Student midwives' knowledge and skills will more often than not be greater than your own. Respect this and work closely with them if the situation arises.

Psychiatry

- Important aspects of the psychiatric history

- Review of the mental state examination

- Core topics

Psychiatric attachments are often less regimented, which allows you greater freedom to divide your time up in a way that you feel is most productive. We would strongly suggest that you try to fully clerk a psychiatric patient every day. Try to take a full history and then perform a mental state examination. Your aim is to build a collection of cases which covers the main conditions tested in psychiatric finals (see core topics, below). A larger proportion of these cases should be those which are more likely to come up in finals, ie depression, schizophrenia, anxiety disorders, eating disorders and personality disorders.

It is due to the relative freedom that psychiatry is often seen as an easy specialty, with great opportunity to sneak off on holiday or catch up on other subjects. We strongly encourage you to maximize the unique opportunity to clerk psychiatric patients and gain an in-depth working knowledge of the main conditions tested in finals. If in your course psychiatry is tested as a station in your final exams, then this is pretty much your only chance to hone your history taking and mental state examination on actual patients.

If psychiatry is one of your final attachments in the few months leading up to finals and there is the potential to compress, for example, four to six weeks allocated to the specialty into three or four weeks while still covering the core conditions to the same depth, then you can create an extra two weeks to revise gaps in the other specialties.

> I failed my psychiatric attachment and had to retake the year as my poor attendance record and borderline performance in the final examination were deemed unacceptable by the examiners.
>
> SR, final-year medical student

The psychiatric history

The psychiatric history is unique, and you should invest time in learning how to take a rapid but thorough psychiatric history for each of the main conditions listed above. Important aspects of the psychiatric history are:

- Aetiology of disease:
  - Childhood support;
  - Home environmental;
  - Genetic factors, for example family history (bio-psychosocial model of disease).
- Significant life events/stressors as precipitants of disease or of flares/ exacerbations;
- Maintaining factors:
  - Recreational drug and alcohol use;
  - High levels of expressed emotion;
  - Poor compliance with therapy or medication.
- Screen for diseases which are differentials of psychiatric conditions, ie organic disorders, for example, hypothyroidism, hypoadrenal, Addison's and chronic alcohol intoxication;
- Effect of the disease on:
  - Occupation;
  - Immediate family: is the patient a main carer for somebody else?
- Forensic history.

Review of the mental state examination

The mental state examination is definitely an art, incorporating a multitude of observations and no actual physical contact with the patient. With practice this can be done fairly rapidly. Separate out your observations from your questions. The example list shown below is for a hypothetical patient suffering from depressive disorder. As with most things in medicine, there are many different ways to remember the list, and one commonly quoted mnemonic is ABCSMITH:

Appearance:
- Appropriately dressed, cleanliness, posture.

Behaviour:
- Facial expression, aggression, agitation, paucity of movement, preoccupied.

Cooperation:
- Eye contact.

Speech:
- Rate;
- Volume;
- Content – form and pattern.

Mood:
- Subjective:
  - 'How is your mood at the moment?'
  - Include suicide risk – 'Have you ever felt like it's all too much and you want to end things?'
- Objective: apathetic, irritable, labile, optimistic, pessimistic.

Insight:
- 'Do you feel you need help with the issues we have discussed today?'

Thoughts:
- Flight of ideas;
- Delusions:
  - 'Do you ever believe things that other people don't?'
  - 'Do you ever think you are being controlled by someone else?'

Hallucinations:

- Do you ever see things that other people don't see?

Core topics

The core topics are listed below with a brief outline of particularly important areas:

- Depression and bipolar disorder, including depression in the elderly:
  - Epidemiology. Greater prevalence in economically deprived urban areas with high unemployment.
  - Triggering factors. Adverse life events such as bereavement, separation from long-term partner, loss of a job and childbirth (in postpartum subtype).
  - Brown's vulnerability factors in working-class women – three or more children under 14 years, no work outside the home and no confiding relationship.
  - Maintaining factors. Unemployment, disability and substance abuse.
  - Presenting symptoms:
    — Psychiatric – anhedonia, guilt, pessimism, suicidal thoughts, delusions of guilt or illness;
    — Physical – low energy, early-morning wakening, decreased libido, change in appetite;
    — Mental – poor concentration, poor memory.
  - Major differentials and associated investigations needed to exclude them: drugs (many drugs have been implicated, and include steroids, Parkinsonian medications such as L-dopa, Alzheimer's medications such as donepezil and beta-blockers such as bisoprolol), alcohol, schizophrenia, hypothyroidism, anxiety disorders and dementia.
  - Features of mania and the commonly used mood-stabilizing drugs such as lithium, carbamazepine and sodium valproate in terms of side effect profile and need for monitoring.
  - Postpartum depression – the spectrum of the 'blues', depression and psychosis.
  - Treatment:
    — Medications – acute, maintenance and prophylaxis phases, comparison of SSRI and tricyclic drugs in terms of safety in overdose, common side effects and cost;
    — Electropsychological treatment (ECT) – overview of the technique and effect on monoamine function, indications and typical treatment regime;

— Psychosocial treatments – understand the role of cognitive behavioural therapy and its effectiveness particularly with negative symptoms such as guilt, pessimism and self-blame. Recognize the importance of ongoing financial, emotional and housing problems as maintaining factors.

- Schizophrenia:
  - Epidemiology. Understand the principles of selective migration and social drift.
  - Aetiology. Evidence of a significant genetic component, neurodevelopmental hypothesis involving gestational factors and early childhood environment.
  - Triggering factors. Significant life events, both positive and negative.
  - Maintaining factors. High levels of expressed emotion in their environment and recreational drug use.
  - Common positive and negative symptoms.
  - ICD10 Diagnostic criteria.
  - Schneider's first rank symptoms. Be able to give examples of the most common, for example thought insertion, delusions of control and bizarre delusions.
  - Major differentials divided into those that can mimic positive symptoms such as psychotic depression and those that mimic negative symptoms such as an acute depressive episode.
  - Subtypes of schizophrenia including paranoid, catatonic and simple.
  - Poor prognostic factors. Divided into patient factors (young male who is socially isolated, uses recreational drugs frequently and is poorly compliant with medications) and illness factors (slow onset of predominantly negative symptoms which respond poorly to treatment and last for a long duration).
  - Treatment:
    — Medications. Commonly prescribed antipsychotic drugs, their effects on positive symptoms, the indications for clozapine, the importance of a long maintenance phase and the advantages and disadvantages of depot injections.
    — Psychosocial. Cognitive behavioural therapy is increasingly used to change the way patients perceive their delusions and the way they react to them. Greater emphasis is placed on ensuring a supportive living environment with either family or friends, and regular occupational therapy to assist them with learning the skills needed to live independently.

- Eating disorders: bulimia and anorexia:
  - Significant overlap with respect to triggers and maintaining factors.
  - Treatment aims.

- Cognitive behavioural therapy has a significant role in changing the extreme body image and fear of being overweight. It aims to modify the learned responses to food and eating.
- SSRIs have a minor role in bulimia as an additional appetite suppressant.

● Dementia and pseudodementia: Alzheimer's disease, vascular dementia, Lewy body dementia and Pick's disease:

- Identify the discriminatory factors which will enable you to answer MCQs based on diagnosis of different types of dementia.

● Old age psychiatry. Understand the different presentations, trigger and maintaining factors and treatment options in the elderly patient suffering from depression or schizophrenia. Dementia becomes increasingly important to rule out and may sometimes coexist. Polypharmacy is common and complicates treatment options.

● Personality disorders:

- Learn the ICD10 clusters of disorders, which, although criticized as being too rigid, form the basis of an initial diagnosis.
- Be aware of the role of the childhood environment in shaping personality disorders.
- In a history station ask about any early displays of the personality traits in question, whether there are significant effects on the type or length of jobs held, and whether there have been any difficulties forming and maintaining close relationships with friends and partners.
- Management strategies include an extra 'crisis' tool which seeks to aid patients who feel things have spiralled out of control and need some additional guidance and help with daily activities.

● Anxiety disorders: obsessive-compulsive disorder, anxiety disorders, post-traumatic stress disorder, adjustment disorders and dissociative disorders:

- Learn a clear example of each.
- Understand the importance of psychological treatments which include stimulus control and exposure/response prevention for OCD, behavioural therapy in the treatment of phobic anxiety disorders, and cognitive therapy which can be applied to most types of anxiety disorders.
- Drug treatments such as antidepressants can help to reduce the frequency and severity of panic attacks. Beta-blockers are occasionally prescribed for symptomatic relief of palpitations in anxiety disorder. Short courses of benzodiazepines are often prescribed to highly distressed patients.

- Mental Capacity Act and sections:
  - Allow patients to be admitted and treated against their will only if they have a mental disorder (includes mental illness, psychopathic disorder and mental impairment).
  - Understand the difference between sections 2 and 3, that they both require two doctors and an approved social worker.
  - Recognize the limits, which are that no treatment can be given outside hospital, and that compulsory treatment can only be given for the mental disorder, ie you cannot use a section to force a patient to undergo a surgical treatment even if they are refusing it secondary to a mental disorder.
  - Understand the test for capacity and be able to describe it succinctly.

- Drugs. Have an understanding of the commonly used psychiatric medications in terms of their indications, common side-effect profile and safety in overdosage:
  - Antidepressants: SSRI, tricyclic and MAOI classes, potentially fatal effects of tricyclic overdose compared to the relative safety of an SSRI overdose. Hypertensive crisis resulting from MAOIs and either tyramine-containing foods or drugs such as amphetamine and SSRIs.
  - Antipsychotic drugs. Typical and atypical classes vary greatly in their mechanism of action but are not significantly more efficacious apart from clozapine, which has a risk of causing agranulocytosis. Atypical antipsychotics have a much lower incidence of extrapyramidal side effects which include acute dystonia, akathisia, Parkinsonian symptoms and tardive dyskinesias.
  - Neuroleptic malignant syndrome and serotonin syndrome – understand the similarity of clinical presentation, the different drug causes and the different treatments.
  - Lithium – learn the therapeutic and supratherapeutic side effects and importance of drug monitoring.
  - Understand that for a large proportion of anxiety disorders drugs are an adjunct but are of secondary importance to psychotherapy in terms of long-term treatment of the symptoms.

Management of any psychiatric condition entails a multidisciplinary approach led by the psychiatric consultant and involving the general practitioner, hospital psychiatric nurses, community psychiatric nurses, crisis response team and care workers.

You should take special care to mention your understanding of the chronic nature of most of the above conditions, the number of different services which are involved in each patient's care, both hospital and community based.

Classification of psychiatric disease is mainly descriptive, not straightforward, and made more confusing through the use of two different systems. The World Health Organization produced ICD-10 (International classification of disease) and the American Psychiatric Association produced the DSM-IV (Diagnostic and statistical manual of mental disorders). They are both widely used, with the DSM-IV having a greater role in research and the ICD-10 being more commonly used clinically. When deciding which system to use for your revision, you should take your lead from your medical school notes and core textbooks, bearing in mind that ICD-10 is the more commonly used system in the UK.

Dermatology

- Learning opportunities

- Core topics

- Skin examination

This specialty is another of those which can sometimes be overlooked as you may not be allocated to it as an individual specialty. Although it may not be on the forefront of the revising student's mind, it does feature prominently in medical finals in the written exams. Furthermore, a skin examination OSCE has been reported as coming up in finals by students from multiple medical schools, and is therefore a skill which you should perfect before your exams.

Learning opportunities

Clinics remain the best chance to examine the large spectrum of conditions. You may get the opportunity to clerk patients before they are seen by the doctor, and then present your findings. If this is the case, make the most of the opportunity.

Even if you are just sitting in, listen to the interaction of the doctor with the patient, and listen to the key questions which are asked, including questions regarding systemic disease. However, another resource you can take advantage of is reading through patient notes while waiting. This will allow you to pick up on elements such as risk factors, which patients are commonly asked about.

GP placements are a great opportunity to see common and chronic skin pathology. You may see first-hand conditions which are listed below, and get an idea of the first-line treatments in the community. Remember to quiz your GP about side effects of important medications; important examples include Roaccutane treatment for acne.

Look for out for treatments which are delivered in clinic, such as application of liquid nitrogen to solar keratoses. You may get to see excisions of small lesions;

rather than just passively absorbing information; try to ask the dermatologist about the condition and its differential diagnoses.

Core topics

You should be aware of the following conditions for your medical school finals. Conditions to look for in the GP setting in particular include:

- Eczema;
- Psoriasis;
- Acne;
- Rosacea;
- Contact dermatitits;
- Solar keratoses;
- Chronic leg ulceration.

Malignancies:

- Basal cell carcinoma;
- Malignant melanoma;
- Squamous cell carcinoma;
- Paget's disease;
- Bowen's disease.

Dermatological emergencies which you should be able to recognize and know the treatment for include:

- Anaphylaxis and angiodema;
- Cutaneous manifestions of meningitis;
- Stevens-Johnson syndrome;
- Necrotizing fascitis.

Conditions which you may see in clinic:

- Pityriasis versicolour;
- Erthyema multiforme and its various causes;

- Café au lait spots;
- Vitiligo;
- Neurofibromatosis;
- Pemphigus and pemphigoid.

Skin examination

- A full skin examination also involves the scalp, mouth, eyes and nails.
- Start by exposing the patient, but maintaining modesty as far as possible.
- Take a systematic approach:
  - A *top-down* approach involves starting with the head and scalp and working down;
  - An *outside-in* approach starts with limbs and works in to the trunk and head.
- Examine each lesion you find for the following characteristics:
  - Topography; is the lesion raised or flat?
  - Colour.
  - Size.
  - Shape/symmetry.
  - Pain.
  - Temperature.

Hints:

- In the assessment of size, look on the desks in your OSCE station for a small ruler. If present, ensure that you measure the lesions.
- If there are very many similar lesions, be sensible with the time and examine one thoroughly as an example of the others. However, be careful for patients with multiple pathologies.
- If there is a raised lump, you should also check it for translucency and fluctuance.

Opthalmology

- How to make the most of your attachment
- Ophthalmoscopy/fundoscopy examination
- Core topics

An ophthalmology attachment in medical school may have its own dedicated time space, or it may be integrated into medical or other subspecialty placements. Making the most of this attachment is important, as written questions on this subject are frequently found in finals, as well as OSCE stations involving real patients, as well as images or models of fundoscopy. There are several manifestations of systemic disease in the eye, as well as a range of eye emergencies which you should be very familiar with.

How to make the most of your attachment

The main form of learning will be attendance at ophthalmology outpatient clinics. This is a wonderful opportunity to see the range of chronic eye pathology. In particular, you should be trying to hone your examination skills, and start to recognize important clinical signs. You may also have the opportunity to discuss the further investigation and management of the patients with the attending specialist.

You may be able to borrow an ophthalmoscope from the department for practice on your colleagues. This represents an invaluable opportunity; do not let it slip by! Most students have limited practice with the device and the examination itself, and as with any OSCE, repetition and practice are the key to success.

Start by familiarizing yourself with the ins and outs of the device, and pay attention to the degree to which you need to change the focus in order to visualize the retina sharply; you may wish to make a note of this, although you may be faced with a different brand in the exam setting. Practise by having someone set the focus off from your ideal setting, so that you can learn how to quickly reset it in the midst of an examination.

Ophthalmoscopy/fundoscopy examination

The examination sequence is as follows:

- Warn the patient about the conditions of the examination: 'During this exam, I will need to shine a light into your eye, and come quite close to your face.'

- Elicit the red reflex by directing light from the ophthalmoscope into the patient's eye from 50 cm away, and viewing the retina through the device. If there is some opacity, this can indicate a cataract.

- Hold your ophthalmoscope correctly, and use your little finger to gauge the space between your face and the patient's.

- Look for the optic disc by tracing the blood vessels to their origin.

- Move towards the midline to visualize the macula.

- After this, examine each of four quadrants in turn, looking at the vessels as well as the retina.

- After you finish, thank the patient, and inform the examiner that you would like to complete your examination with an assessment of the patient's visual acuity with a Snellen chart and an assessment of their oculomotor function.

Hints:

- You may need to adjust the dioptre in order to focus sharply on the retina.

- In an OSCE setting, you may find that the room lights are quite bright. Look for a light switch, but ask permission from the examiner to dim the lights.

- Always examine the normal eye first.

Core topics

Conditions to be aware of for finals can be considered in terms of different presentations:

Acute visual loss:
- Retinal artery or vein occlusion;
- Optic neuritis;
- Retinal detachment;
- ARMD (age-related macular degeneration – wet);
- Ischaemic optic neuropathy.

The 'red eye':
- Conjunctivitis;
- Keratitis;
- Episcleritis;
- Scleritis;
- Anterior uveitis;
- Endopthalmitis;
- Acute closed angle glaucoma.

Slow visual loss:

- Cataract;
- Open angle glaucoma;
- ARMD (dry);
- Diabetic retinopathy;
- Refractive error.

Other acute eye emergencies:

- Chemical injury: common dangerous agents, treatment;
- Trauma: including traumatic hyphaema and orbital fractures;
- Penetrating trauma: management of a residual intraocular foreign body.

Miscellaneous:

- Ectropion;
- Lumps; Chalazion, hordeolum.

Summary

- It is important to realize that the five major specialties differ hugely in terms of the type of knowledge required, type of examination performed and format of final exams.

- Standard attachment timetables usually aim to give you a wide coverage of most aspects of a specialty but may not focus sufficiently on those areas you are likely to be examined in. Be aware of what these areas are from your first week and adjust your timetable accordingly.

- The standard history and examination for a medical clerking has to be modified for each specialty and we highlight the main differences for paediatrics, obstetrics, gynaecology and psychiatry.

- There are core conditions in each specialty to which you should devote more time to learning.

- Don't assume that the final exams in each specialty will be similar to each other or to your final medical exams. In most medical schools, the format of specialty exams is likely to differ in terms of written material (MCQ vs EMQ vs essay vs short-answer papers) and clinical examination (OSCE vs short cases vs simulations vs viva stations).

CHAPTER 3

Improving your learning technique

In order to maximize your uptake from any given learning opportunity, it is important to have an understanding of the different ways in which we learn new skills and acquire knowledge. There are a great number of theories, many of which are complicated and not directly relevant. We have chosen a few with the sole purpose of illustrating our core message, which is that you should take a **considered approach** to your learning.

We will cover how to apply these theories to the way that you approach a particular learning scenario. We will discuss new methods of 'input' other than the traditional means of bookwork. We will cover how best to consolidate knowledge and draw links to distant material. We discuss some alternative hospital-based work which supports the more standard approach of hospital-based learning. We explain how teaching is often a 'win–win' activity and go over the importance of a learning environment.

The learning cycle

Students should seek to challenge the traditional model comprising an input (lectures or reading a book) which leads to knowledge uptake, which is then formally tested (exam or viva). Methods of assessment are continually evolving, with most medical school finals involving a combination of knowledge-based assessment through a selection of written papers and skills-based assessment through a selection of OSCE stations. The response to a changing assessment process should be to adapt the traditional process through which we acquire knowledge and skills.

One attempt to break down the learning process was described by Kolb and Fry (1975), and describes a four-stage learning cycle where 'experiences' lead to 'reflections' which are then condensed into 'concepts'. These shape new actions which are 'actively tested' in order to form new experiences. While this artificial division of the learning cycle is argued by some to be too rigid, it nonetheless serves as a starting point to examine the way in which we learn. One important message here is that students should allow time for the 'reflection' and 'concept' phases. We are often pushed too rapidly from the 'experience' of stage one to the 'active testing' of stage four without allowing sufficient time to think through the concepts and knowledge gained through the experience. By considering the experience, students should be able to form links with distant material, better understand the material presented, and synthesize the material into a personal format which is more memorable and robust.

A worked example is shown below:

1 Concrete experience – attend a lecture on the management of an acute exacerbation of asthma.

2 Observation and reflection – spend time reading not only about asthma, but also about related presentations of breathlessness such as pneumothorax, pneumonia, cardiac failure and anaphylaxis.

3 Abstract concepts – consider how these other conditions could mimic the presentation of asthma, and which are the main discriminatory factors in terms of pathology, presentation and treatment.

4 Actively test – using a patient presenting with breathlessness as an example, either imagine the case, be questioned by a colleague about it, or clerk such a patient. Try to work through the list of differential diagnoses using your earlier reflections on the similarities and differences of the various conditions which may mimic asthma.

Learning scenarios and new input modalities

Students should seek to test different methods of gaining skills and knowledge. First, you should understand that different teaching scenarios utilize a different proportion of the various input modalities; namely visual, auditory, kinaesthetic and 'reading–writing'. Visual learners often understand a concept best when it is presented in a written or visually engaging format. Auditory learners may prefer a concept to be explained to them, and then to discuss it as a group. Kinaesthetic learners prefer to engage in experiments or to interact with real patients. While most students have grown accustomed to a particular type of input, they may find that after 10 years of learning through reading a textbook they actually understand and retain far more information through a learning scenario with a greater auditory component, for example in group discussions.

Examples of the common learning scenarios with their various input modalities are shown below:

TABLE 3.1 Learning scenarios and input modalities

Learning scenario	Input modality
Lecture	Visual, auditory, writing
Lecture notes	Reading–writing
Reading textbooks	Reading–writing
Group discussion	Auditory
Experiment	Visual, kinaesthetic
Clerking and presenting a patient	Visual, auditory, kinaesthetic, writing
Attending outpatient clinics	Visual, auditory, kinaesthetic

One tip from the list above is that the hospital-based activities are a much more rounded learning experience, involving many more sensory modalities; hence the oft-quoted advice to clerk a patient, present them and then read up on the case immediately afterwards.

> I always assumed that I was predominantly a visual learner but since engaging in group discussions and activities such as clerking patients, I realize that I respond well to auditory and kinaesthetic inputs. I now actively build these elements into my revision schedule.
>
> DY, fourth-year medical student

From this we can add a few less commonly used tools which access some of the equally effective but less obvious sensory inputs:

1 Listening to a recording of a lecture uses the auditory input. Many students find this an extremely time-effective learning tool as you can listen to lectures while commuting or carrying out daily activities.

2 Brainstorming or question-and-answer sessions with a colleague also use the auditory input but are a much more active process and often have the advantage of creating stronger memories.

3 Simulation with a colleague or mannequin to practise examination routines uses visual and kinaesthetic elements to create strong memories and associations. It sounds very obvious, but many students fall into the trap of trying to learn examination routines by reading about them. It is far more effective to practise performing an examination than read about it (see Chapter 7 for more tips on different simulation types).

I find that a 15-minute Q&A session is a welcome break from reading, and rapidly identifies my weak areas.

LK, final-year medical student

The above list is by no means exhaustive, and students should be open to trying each type of teaching scenario.

Individual students often have a preference for a particular learning style but should be open to new learning styles which incorporate more input modalities.

Consolidating knowledge through reinforcement

Having learnt about a condition or an examination routine, it is important to consider how best to consolidate the knowledge and also how to build on it and draw links with other material.

There are several ways to consolidate your knowledge, and certainly repetition is a core theme. What you should consider is that there are different ways to carry out repetition, all aiming to strengthen what is initially a single-track path that is difficult to find through all the long grass, and to turn it into a big road which is rapidly found and easily navigable.

When trying to consolidate knowledge such as a topic you have read, some of the options are to reread the material, write some brief notes, dictate some notes (and then listen to the notes within the next few days), discuss the material in a question-and-answer format with a friend or undergo self-testing through past papers or online questions.

Repetition should be moulded to fit your particular course. For example, if you have a series of lectures you could try reading the lecture notes the day before, attending the lecture, and then discussing the material with a friend or reading the material from a different source. While the above approach sounds time consuming, once you start a system and get used to it you should be able to carry each part out fairly rapidly. The great strength of repetition over a short time frame is to quickly overlay paths in your memory to facilitate recall at a later date.

> I now have a system where I skim through the lecture notes the night before, and then read the notes again after the lecture. It doesn't take much time but my retention of the material is far higher.
>
> WH, final-year medical student

Breaking down the above example, the pre-reading of the lecture notes allows you to familiarize yourself with the topic. Your time in the lecture is made more valuable as, instead of spending time trying to understand the core subject material, you can give the lecturer your full attention and absorb the more subtle or difficult points which they are trying to explain. The post-lecture reading, which may incorporate other sources such as online resources or textbooks, serves to fill in any gaps which were not covered in the lecture, and also to reinforce the material once more.

Building bridges

Actively try to build mental bridges between related topics. In the same manner as using mind maps as an aid for essays, try to work out which conditions link in with your core topic and then read the aspects of your linked topics that relate to your core topic. While this may sound complex and laborious, we can illustrate it with a worked example using inflammatory bowel disease:

- Read lecture notes on inflammatory bowel disease to learn core aspects of the symptoms, signs, investigations and treatment.

- Attend the lecture or workshop, or complete the problem-based learning module, during which you gain understanding of the difficult concepts such as how the pathology relates to the complications, reinforce core concepts and learn additional material such as the scoring system for calculating the severity of an acute flare, the advanced treatment options or the extra-articular manifestations.

- Reread the lecture notes and explore other written material to consolidate all the knowledge gained so far and build links to other relevant topics such as other causes of altered bowel habit, lower gastrointestinal bleeding or lower abdominal pain.

The importance lies in the real-world nature of this stage of learning; real cases are never 'textbook' or 'classic' in nature, and the ability to rapidly compare and contrast your main diagnosis with the main differentials will greatly enhance your diagnostic skills as a clinician.

Reinforcement is a vital learning tool and you should try to actively incorporate it into the way you learn.

The 'hidden curriculum'

The differences between a syllabus and a curriculum are described by many authors, but with particular relevance to medical student finals, you can think of them as being an outline of the course material and a series of learning activities and outcomes. Although we describe a sample curriculum in Chapter 13, this is really more along the lines of a syllabus as it outlines the information you will need to know. In contrast, this book as a whole functions more as a curriculum; almost all chapters describe learning tasks which you can undertake to support your learning.

However, many students are not familiar with the 'hidden curriculum' of the medical school, a concept first coined by Jackson (1968), who referred to this in terms of general education. This describes the spectrum of learning activities which you can undertake, which are not specified by the medical school itself. For example, in learning and presenting imaging (Chapter 10), students are not specifically told to go and study plenty of normal chest X-rays on wards, but as we describe, actively looking for these learning opportunities allows you to identify pathological imaging much more rapidly and correctly.

Other examples include ophthalmoscopy practice on fellow students (Chapter 7) or attending post-mortems when well prepared, to discuss the underlying pathology of patients (Chapter 2). Take advantage of the range of non-standard or 'hidden curriculum' items we describe in each chapter to gain the most out of your final medical school year; as you will find, the most savvy students are already doing this.

Social learning theory

Principles of peer-assisted learning may come into play for medical school finals, and the dialogue between peers within a learning activity may be particularly useful here. We can consider this in terms of Vygotsky's (1978) social cultural theory of learning. He describes a 'zone of proximal development' which represents the potential learning areas which could be achieved by a student with sufficient guidance and support. A group of peers may exhibit variable rates of progression, and therefore peers who are further ahead may fall into the zone of proximal development of less-advanced peers, and so be able to help them with their development in this area. However, teachers and doctors may be so far ahead of the student that they do not fall within this zone. Essentially, fellow students may be the best teachers for other students as they are closer to their level, but moreover, they themselves will also benefit from teaching, as they consolidate and organize the material in their minds.

How does this apply to medical school finals? It is particularly helpful to consider **simulations** described in Chapter 7 as an opportunity for peer-assisted learning. We have suggested different ways of practising OSCEs using fellow students as models for examination. You will be able to reinforce your own knowledge by teaching others, as well as performing self-assessment of your own position by working in a group of students at a similar level.

The environment and its effect on recall

Egstrom et al (1972) and Godden and Baddeley (1975) investigated the role of environment on recall by placing cohorts of learners in underwater or above-water environments. They found through their unusual experiments that the environment in which you learn information may affect your ability to remember it, and therefore this is important to medical students as the different papers are undertaken in different environments.

For example, MCQ papers are often taken in large examination halls, whereas OSCEs are undertaken in simulated ward environments. A simple way to optimize your learning environment is to focus your clinical examination setting in the ward environment, while, on the other hand, revising written work at your own desk may better emulate the conditions in which you will be tested. However, you may be able take advantage of this difference in recall in more sophisticated ways, such as learning for written examinations in quiet groups of peers and undertaking mini-mock exams or MCQ practice together. This will allow you to get a feel for the pressures exerted in such environments, and give you an edge in terms of recall performance. It has the obvious additional benefit of having many students around at the end of the practice, to discuss performance as well as answers.

Summary

- Try to use a more thoughtful, considered approach to any learning opportunity.

- Be aware of the different input modalities.

- Critically analyse your current learning style to see which input modalities you generally favour, and also whether you could benefit from the addition of a different input modality.

- Try to work out which description of learner type best applies to you so that you can both focus on situations which work best for you and also avoid commonly associated problems.

- Test yourself in an active manner to identify areas which may need further reinforcement.

- Build reinforcement into your routine so that you go over the same material in different ways over a short time frame.

- Take time to think about what you have just learnt, and actively draw links with relevant material.

- Make the most of opportunities in the 'hidden curriculum' described in this book.

- Social learning activities such as simulations (Chapter 7) or even group study for MCQs, help everyone within the group.

- Focusing your learning activities in the appropriate environments may aid your recall.

References

Egstrom, GG, Weltman, G, Baddeley, AD, Cuccaro, WJ, and Willis, MA (1972) *Underwater work performance and work tolerance*. Report no 51, Bio-Technology Laboratory, University of California, Los Angeles

Godden, AR and Baddley, AD (1975) *Context-dependant memory in two natural environments; on land and underwater*. British Journal of Psychology, 66 (3): 325–31

Jackson, PW (1968) *Life in Classrooms*. Holt, Rinehart and Winston

Kolb, DA and Fry, R (1975) 'Toward an applied theory of experiential learning', in C Cooper (ed.) *Theories of Group Process*, London:John Wiley

Vygotsky, L (1978) *Mind in Society: Development of Higher Psychological Processes*, p. 86. Harvard University Press

CHAPTER 4

The final six months

The mind-numbing 'realization' of finals is well described and while it may hit some candidates months before, many will experience it in the two weeks before the exams commence. It is vital not to get distracted and scared by the impending exams. We will outline how to build a revision timetable for the six months leading up to finals in the hope that by the time the fear strikes, you have completed the majority of your revision. We will concentrate mainly on the last month as this is where many students find they lose their sense of direction and focus. We will also discuss some practical aspects of what to take and wear to the exam. We will go through some tips to remain focused and use the stress in a positive manner.

Revision timetables

Revision timetables vary hugely from very complex and detailed multipage documents accounting for every working hour to more vague plans detailing subjects to be covered but not the actual topics. The most important thing to note is that we each work differently. Some students will prefer the first example as the entire syllabus is accounted for and time allocated accordingly, whilst other students find it too inflexible and regimented. Despite the variability in how different students construct their revision timetables, we encourage every finals student to plan a timetable, even if it turns out to be as non-specific as 'Monday – medicine, Tuesday – surgery, Wednesday – specialties, Thursday – OSCEs', etc. The core principles are:

● Start early; definitely give yourself six months to prepare.

● Flexibility is key. Needing to rewrite the timetable after two weeks is a sign not of failure but of the fact that you are fine-tuning the timetable to suit your work patterns and knowledge base.

● Think carefully about your existing knowledge base, strengths and weaknesses, and weight the time allocated to different topics accordingly. Examples of this are:

  – If you happen to have read and understood a lot of respiratory and gastrointestinal medicine, then it shouldn't take too long to refresh your memory. Time saved here could be shifted to another subject which you feel will require additional time to understand and retain.

  – If your cardiac, respiratory and abdominal examinations are slick and require only a polish, then spend more time on your neurological and rheumatological examinations to bring them up to the same standard.

  – If your examination routines are of a consistently high quality, spend more time honing your presentation of clinical findings.

Don't forget that the examination finishes with your presentation of the key findings to the examiner. This is a common area which is poorly prepared yet so easily practised.

● Your natural work patterns should be integral to the design of the timetable, which essentially means thinking through a typical study day starting with the time you expect to begin working, when you break for lunch and dinner, and how long you want to work for in total. Consider breaking down each three-to-four-hour session into shorter one-hour blocks. Despite your best intentions to work for three hours solidly, the majority of students are not able to do so and at least one hour in three is generally wasted through boredom or loss of concentration.

● Appreciate the concept of 'gears', which is essentially that you can only sustain a period of maximally intense revision over approximately two weeks. If we call this fifth gear, then between starting your finals revision at a time six months prior, when you will be in first gear, you should gradually push yourself forwards in noticeable increments, advancing through gears one to five in terms of time and effort spent on revision.

● You should also take into account which attachments you have over the final six months. Most students will have at least a month of general medicine and general surgery. Try to concentrate on the attachment to which you are posted.

For example, when doing general surgery you have special access to surgical wards, clinics and assessment units and should take advantage of this by examining lots of patients and reviewing lots of surgical conditions. You should try to consolidate the surgical conditions in your mind during your reading time.

● Building in 'buffers' can be helpful in time management. These are areas of time towards the end of the day which are left empty, to allow shifts due to unexpected circumstances. For example, if you build a one-hour buffer into your timetable and find that revising the causes of pulmonary fibrosis took longer than you thought, you will be able to shift your learning activities along in time, and fill the buffer at the end of the day. If you do not have any fluctuations, you can use the buffer for additional work or relaxation.

> One of the most valuable reasons for constructing a revision timetable is to focus your mind on the mammoth task ahead.

We strongly advise that with six months to go, you try to 'buddy up' with one or more colleagues who are ideally of similar motivation to you and with the same goals. You can support each other through this intensely stressful period by sharing advice from other sources, daily question-and-answer sessions to test material learnt that day, working together occasionally to motivate each other, practising examination routines and presenting to each other while taking it in turns to play the role of examiner. However, be aware that as numbers of students rise, it becomes more difficult to remain focused and the overall efficiency decreases. We would suggest no more than three or four to a study group.

I learn a lot through group discussion with friends as they may have attended different revision courses, seen a different spectrum of patients and been taught by different clinicians.

MJ, recent Cardiff graduate

> There is a lot to be gained through cooperative effort, so be careful you don't become isolated over the months leading up to finals.

One month before

Do not impulsively buy a new book just because you heard it might be good. A panic buy will merely cloud your mind with new ideas, layouts or strategies. If there is truly a core textbook that you were not aware of until now, then you will have to consider buying it, but time is scarce and you won't be able to read through key chapters more than a couple of times. If possible, try to continue with what you have been using – most texts have broadly similar information and you will have subconsciously become used to the layout and style of the one you have been preparing with. Refer to Chapter 14 in this volume for in-depth book reviews.

Take frequent short breaks when you recognize that you aren't processing information effectively – usually after about 45–60 minutes. Even a short walk around the library or to get a drink may be sufficient, and is far better than sitting in front of the same page for 15 minutes. Change your location if you are finding it difficult to concentrate; consider your room, the library, a different library or coffee shop.

Find out from colleagues if there are any last-minute changes to exam times or venue, and if any extra revision lectures or supervisions have been arranged by the medical school. These final revision lectures are often given by the actual examiners or by clinicians who have been invited to set questions, and therefore subconsciously their material may reflect some aspects of the topics they have submitted.

Use the stress and nervous energy to read with renewed enthusiasm and focus. You may be pleasantly surprised by how long you are now able to concentrate and by how much you are retaining from every topic you read. Your new-found energy could enable you to create a new revision timetable with increased study hours per day. Try to include high-yield topics which have a high chance in appearing in your finals or that you personally feel weaker in.

> I always surprise myself by how well I am able to focus in the month before an exam... I can usually study for far longer periods and find I retain much more information.
>
> AJ, foundation-year doctor

A list drawn from a survey of recent candidates shows that some topics are commonly felt to be either poorly understood or suitable for last-minute revision for other reasons, such as being difficult to retain or frequently tested, and are listed below:

Cardiology:

- Valvular disease. Revise the common valve lesions and their main discriminatory clinical signs.

– Acute coronary syndrome. Acute management including indications for primary coronary intervention and thrombolysis. Risk factors for coronary disease, TIMI scoring and the treatment of non-ST elevation ACS.

– Acute heart failure. Typical presenting features, precipitants, classic features on chest radiograph and management priorities.

– Arrhythmias. Principles of management of tachy- and bradyarrhythmias.

– Common ECG abnormalities – cardiac ischaemia and infarction, bundle branch block, findings in pulmonary embolus and hyperkalaemia.

Respiratory:

– Bronchiectasis – common causes, clinical symptoms and signs, management strategies.

– Bronchial carcinoma – common types, complications divided into local, metastatic and endocrine.

– Pneumothorax – different management strategies depending on whether it is a primary or secondary type. Theory of the insertion of intercostal chest drains.

– Pleural effusion. How to distinguish between an exudate and a transudate and common causes of each.

– Interstitial lung disease – simple classification and definitions.

– COPD – typical findings on examination, management of an acute exacerbation.

– Asthma – BTS guidelines for chronic asthma and the BTS guidelines for the management of an acute exacerbation.

– Pneumonia – atypical types and discriminatory factors, complications.

Gastroenterology:

– Acute upper and lower GI bleed – priorities of resuscitation, early endoscopy for variceal bleeds, options including proton pump inhibitors, FFP and vitamin K.

– Liver failure – common causes and investigations.

– Inflammatory bowel disease – presentation and management of a flare, features of a severe flare.

– Diarrhoea and or vomiting – differentials, both medical and surgical.

Neurology:

– Revise the dermatomes and myotomes.

– Subarachnoid haemorrhage – classic presentation, features on CT and treatment options.

– Meningitis – classic history and physical signs, immediate treatment and LP findings.

- Stroke and TIA – different cerebral artery territories, CT findings, indications for thrombolysis and $ABCD_2$ score.
- Subdural and extradural haemorrhage – features on CT and typical histories.
- Epilepsy – classification, first-line treatment options for primary generalized and partial seizures.
- Parkinson's disease, Alzheimer's disease, Lewy body dementia and vascular dementia – typical history and clinical findings.
- Multiple sclerosis – typical presentation, clinical findings, different forms of disease, diagnostic tests and treatment options.
- Motor neurone disease – main forms and spectrum of clinical signs.
- Myasthenia gravis – pathophysiology, typical history, clinical signs, diagnosis and treatment.

Endocrinology:

- Diabetes – micro- and macrovascular complications, management of diabetic ketoacidosis and hyperosmolar hyperketotic state.
- Thyroid disease – common clinical symptoms and signs of hypo- and hyperthyroidism.
- Cushing's syndrome – common causes and pathway of investigations including overnight dexamethasone suppression test, 48-hour dexamethasone suppression test, plasma ACTH and high-dose dexamethasone suppression test.
- Addison's disease – common causes, vague symptom set, signs, classical biochemical disturbance, synacthen test and treatment options.
- Phaeochromocytoma – classic presentation, urinary collection for free catecholamines and treatment.
- Acromegaly – clinical signs, oral glucose tolerance test and treatment both surgical and medical.

Renal medicine:

- Urinary tract infection – common organisms, complications, treatment.
- Renal calculi – presenting symptoms and signs, investigations and treatment.
- Acute renal failure – common causes, initial management and complications, especially hyperkalaemia. Indications for emergency dialysis.

Rheumatology:

- Rheumatoid arthritis – classic examination findings, extra-articular manifestations, diagnostic criteria and treatment options, including DMARDS and their common side effects.

   – Osteoarthritis – typical pattern of pain and joint features.

   – Gout and pseudogout – discriminatory features with respect to joint distribution, common causes and findings on polarized light microscopy.

Haematology:

   – Anaemia – common causes divided by MCV (mean cell volume).

   – Bleeding – common bleeding disorders, treatment of the over-warfarinized patient, complications of transfusion, the range and use of the different blood products available.

   – Myeloma – pathophysiology and classical symptoms, common complications and treatment options.

   – Polycythaemia – relative and absolute types, common causes, polycythaemia rubra vera.

   – Thrombophilia – common inherited causes.

Infectious diseases:

   – Antibiotics – empirical treatment options for the main infections (learn from your regional tertiary hospital antibiotic protocol).

   – Gastroenteritis – spectrum of organisms, differentials based on duration of illness, type of food eaten, incubation period and clinical features.

   – Malaria – life-threatening complications, prognostic features and treatment options.

   – Tuberculosis – diagnosis, treatment regimes, common drug side effects, spread of multidrug-resistant forms.

   – HIV – basic virology, transmission, stages of infection, diagnosis, AIDS, treatment options, association with MDR-TB.

Surgery:

   – See Chapter 2, 'The specialties', which reviews key surgical topics.

> The problem here is with limited time and an overwhelming volume of material. Therefore it is important that you choose carefully to cover the areas that would be most helpful to you.

Two weeks before

The couple of weeks leading up to your exams will be very frightening for most students, as your natural reaction is to feel you need to cover your entire syllabus to be fully prepared, yet you only have a few weeks. It is vital to pause, and focus your efforts on particular areas. Possible strategies are based on a variety of factors which are presented below as a list of questions.

Have you got any 'weak' areas?

Every student has topics or even specialties which either frighten them or bore them, or that they have never quite understood. It is very easy to bury your head in the sand and hope that the areas you haven't covered aren't examined. However, remember that most OSCE examinations allow you to fail only two or three stations, and it is entirely possible that several of your 'weaker' areas come up in the same exam. To guard against this, if you don't already know what they are, you should actively seek out your weaker areas through a combination of reading, question-based assessment and examination so that you can start addressing the deficit. You can also make excellent use of the sample curriculum (Chapter 13) to identify these areas.

> I am glad I didn't choose to bin any subjects, as the topics that came up in finals included a lot of peripheral and less commonly covered areas.
>
> RF, foundation-year doctor

Don't rely on your stronger areas to bring in the marks; you should be able to pass your finals in a hypothetical exam composed entirely of questions and OSCE stations based on your weaker areas.

Have you tried to question spot?

Focus on areas you feel have a high likelihood of being tested this year, whether because they have appeared every year, or perhaps because they haven't appeared for several years.

> I went through the last five years of question papers with a friend and several of our guesses were correct... We subsequently scored very highly on those questions.
>
> DB, Oxford graduate

There is a method to question spotting and you should go through at least the last 10 years of past papers to look for patterns and trends. See Chapter 12, 'Revising for MCQ and EMQ examinations' for further tips.

Do your examination and presentation skills match the strength of your knowledge?

There is still time to remedy this deficiency (see Chapter 7, 'Simulations') through the use of simulations and presenting to colleagues. Practise talking through your examinations while performing them on a simulated patient. In particular, ensure your verbal instructions are as consistent as your physical examination routine. The neurology examination in particular has a large number of instructions and you should rehearse these until you no longer need to actively think of them but can proceed through the examination on autopilot. Another important area to rehearse is the list at the end of each examination, eg 'To complete my examination I would like to...' (refer to Chapter 5, 'OSCE stations', for a review of each system and list of further tests to be requested).

Have you done enough to pass?

Before starting on the minutiae, ensure your knowledge of core topics is consolidated. A good test of a subject area is to perform a memory audit of the main conditions (see Chapter 11, 'Memory audit and differential diagnosis trees'). If you are able to recall 75% or more of the main points of the main conditions, then you have enough knowledge to pass. Refer to the sample curriculum (Chapter 13) for a detailed understanding of which topics are considered core knowledge.

You are far more likely to be considered for a distinction with a well-delivered answer containing core material than with a rambling, hesitant answer containing advanced material.

Are you a distinction candidate?

Truly this is more a particular state of mind and attitude than an innate quality. Gaining a distinction or merit is not as difficult as you might think. We hope that all the way through this book we have exploded the myth behind the mystery that is the 'extra' mark. Now is a good time to concentrate on delivery and style, which count a long way towards those all-important extra marks which, when added up, will form the basis of a distinction.

> I was really surprised to be awarded a distinction for finals as I never thought of myself as top of my class, and certainly didn't know everything about every condition... It paid off to concentrate on presentation of clinical findings and discussion of management plans.
>
> AI, Cambridge graduate

Don't try to examine too many patients at this late stage. Time lost commuting to hospital, searching for patients and then waiting for them to become free will only frustrate you and increase your levels of anxiety. Your time is better spent practising on a friend or imaginary patient, and in any case the wards are often closed to medical students in the weeks leading up to finals.

Days before

There are always some last-minute facts and figures that each of us find particularly difficult to retain for more than a few days. Now is your chance to commit them to your short-term memory. One example is scoring systems such as the CURB65, ABCD2, modified Glasgow, Truelove and Witts criteria and Rockall score. Consider listing the various scoring systems by specialty to aid recall.

> I usually compile a list several months before of key facts and scoring systems that I find particularly difficult to remember so I can put them in my short-term memory a couple of days before my exams.
>
> RC, ACCS trainee

Rapidly leafing through or mentally scanning picture books is a very high-yield activity which works well in the week leading up to your finals. Spend several hours in the medical library browsing through books such as an ophthalmology atlas, medical cases for finals, and a book of surgical signs. You should skim through each book, glancing at the pictures and the condition they represent. These mental snapshots of clinical conditions will last until the exam, and even if only two or three conditions actually feature in your final exams, it is time well spent.

Last-minute reading can be extraordinarily important; never underestimate how often topics read in the days leading up to your finals actually appear in the exam.

Be aware that panic can set in very easily at this late stage. If you find yourself skimming through your notes or books without taking anything in, then stop, take a short break and try to focus again. If you are unable to calm yourself enough to absorb any written material, then switch to a more active process such as a question-and-answer session or practise your examination routines.

Make every effort to reduce stress on the day by checking:

- your route to the venue;
- the time and venue of exams;
- that you have the examination slip, entry code, identification slip.

The night before

One of the most important things you can do is to be well rested, so make an effort to eat well and get a good night's sleep. Take comfort from the previous six months' preparation, and try to relax.

The day of the exam

If you don't know it by now, it really is too late, and anything you read isn't really sinking in at this late stage. The main benefit of reading anything will be to settle your mind and calm yourself.

When you arrive at the examination centre or hospital, don't let yourself be intimidated or put off by people who have just finished. Remember that there are usually a few different OSCE circuits and any patient you hear about may not be on your circuit. Your colleague may also have completely misinterpreted the clinical signs and arrived at the wrong diagnosis. Do whatever makes you most relaxed and focused, be that taking a walk, chatting to friends or skimming through a textbook in the library.

What to wear and take to the exam

Decide what you are going to wear and then make sure everything fits and looks presentable at least a week before. You are aiming to look professional and to blend in with your colleagues. This is definitely not the time to try something new in terms of style or colour, as there is nothing worse on the day than feeling uncomfortable or worried that you look out of place. Men should avoid brightly coloured or highly patterned shirts, and women should avoid low-cut tops or short skirts. Consider tying back long hair to prevent it from falling in front of your face while examining a patient. Whether you are wearing trousers or a skirt, you should be comfortable while kneeling during an abdominal examination. The 'bare below the elbows' policy now applies to examinations as well as wards, and while you may turn up in a suit, be prepared to be asked to take your jacket off. The pre-exam instructions are usually precise in terms of dress code, so read them carefully.

This is not a time to stand out from the crowd because of your unusual choice of clothes.

As a rule, any equipment other than a stethoscope will be provided by the examiners. You should be receptive and note any equipment placed on the table next to an OSCE patient as it is there for a reason, and if you have managed to get to the end of your examination without using it, then it should be the result of a considered decision; for example, testing the dorsal column with proprioception removes the need to use the tuning fork.

What equipment to take:

- stethoscope;
- pen torch;
- pen.

What equipment is unnecessary:

- tendon hammer;
- ophthalmoscope;
- neurotip;

- hat pin;

- cotton wool;

- tuning fork;

- pocket Snellen chart.

> Trying to carry too many items while wearing unfamiliar clothes is a sure way to drop them all on the floor and consequently look amateurish and incompetent.

If it all gets a bit too stressful and you find yourself unable to concentrate, or even worse, feel like you can't face the exam, remember the following:

- You have been training for this moment for six years; you know a lot more and are a lot more competent than you realize.

- At the end of the day it's just an exam, and you can always retake it. Why not just give it a go?

- As opposed to in professional exams, the examiners are really trying to pass you and will often drop extra hints or try to lead you towards the correct diagnosis.

- It is surprising to hear, but many candidates recall actually enjoying their finals. The culmination of many years of preparation is that you now carry more knowledge than you ever will use in your whole medical career, and there is very little that you could face that you won't know a considerable amount about.

Once I got a few cases correct, I started to relax and really relished the opportunity to examine patients with classic signs and then discuss the findings with the examiner.

KJ, St George's graduate

> You have the knowledge required to pass. Try to relax and you may even enjoy the experience!

Summary

- Take time to write a revision timetable which accounts for your attachments in the last few months approaching finals and your work patterns. Don't be deterred if you find you have to rewrite it after the first two weeks.

- Don't become isolated as your revision progresses – form small study groups and talk to your friends to see what they are revising, what methods they are using and if they have heard of any changes to the exam format.

- Be honest with yourself and identify weak areas which need more work.

- Consider writing a new revision timetable for the month before your finals which is focused on high-yield topics.

- Don't neglect the significant practical aspect to finals, which includes honing your examination routine and presenting your findings.

- Identify which books would be useful to scan in the days leading up to the exam.

- Write a list of scoring systems and last-minute facts and figures to learn the week before the exam.

- Triple check exam details – venue, date, time, dress code and equipment needed.

- Arrive early and stay focused but relaxed.

PART TWO

OSCEs

CHAPTER 5

OSCE stations

This chapter is not aimed at teaching you how to perform a standard OSCE-style examination, and neither is it meant to be an exhaustive list of common symptoms/signs; for this information we recommend a formal examination skills book or medical textbook.

It is instead aimed at honing and refining your standard examination techniques, making them slicker and your presentation more elegant, with the end result hopefully boosting a good pass into a distinction or merit.

We will cover common examination pitfalls, examiners' loves and hates, and guide you through a swift but thorough examination style.

Of course this isn't real life, of course it is artificial, but this is the current system and until they find a better way to examine you, you'll have to get used to it. There is certainly no point complaining about it and getting frustrated. In many respects having a standardized and repeatable station that every candidate goes through is much fairer than previous methods of testing.

Examinations are not what the majority of clinicians would perform in real life, so take care to learn the orthodox, standard examinations method from a suitable book (see Chapter 14).

Common pitfalls

- Instructions
- Upsetting the examiner
- Hurting the patient
- Exposure
- Observation
- Presenting your findings
- Making up findings

Instructions

Pay attention to the *exact* instruction given to you. Examples of subtly different instructions are:

'Please examine this patient's heart.'

'Please perform a cardiovascular examination.'

'Please examine the pulse and praecordium of this patient.'

'Please examine the radial pulse and tell us your findings.'

The examiners will then instruct you what else they would like you to examine.

The bottom line is that you should not assume that just because this is a cardio-vascular station you can turn off your brain, operate in automatic and perform your standard examination. Time may be limited, and the examiners may wish you to concentrate on particular aspects of the examination that they know have findings. Be prepared to perform only a small part of the examination; for example, you could be asked to only inspect and auscultate the chest. Carrying out palpation and pulses may only annoy the examiner.

> I tried to get away with too much on my cardiovascular station but the examiner quickly made it apparent that he was annoyed. I then followed all the instructions to the letter and he was happy with my examination.
>
> ND, foundation-year doctor

Listen very carefully to the instruction given; not understanding subtle differences may frustrate the examiner.

Upsetting the examiner

Try to be aware of upsetting, annoying or frustrating your examiner, as they will then have less patience for any mistakes you make. The most common ways to do this are:

- Not listening precisely to the instruction given.

- Trying to get away with too much, for example feeling for peripheral pulses, assessing the JVP and palpating the apex beat when the instruction was 'Listen to this patient's heart.'

- Being too slow, dawdling over peripheral aspects of the examination such as the end of the bed observation or the hands.

- Not being understanding, kind and polite to the patients who have all given up their time to be there, and some of whom may be fairly unwell.

- Failing to demonstrate that you understand how important and serious your finals are through casual remarks such as 'Yeah' or gestures such as standing with your arms folded or leaning against the wall. In many cases students get so stressed during finals that they revert to reflex behavioural patterns, which unfortunately tend to be the more casual type.

You may occasionally not understand the instruction, in which case it is reasonable to ask the examiner to clarify or rephrase the question.

Be aware of your body language and posture as you may inadvertently annoy the examiner.

Hurting the patient

You must never, ever cause a patient any discomfort or pain. It is a sign that either your examination technique is too rough, you did not adequately explain to the patient what you were going to do, or you did not find out at the start of the examination if there were any painful areas. If the patient shows any sign of flinching or discomfort, the examiner will look upon this very harshly.

> Ask the patient if there are any painful areas, warn them before you perform any joint movements, and be extremely gentle at all times.

Exposure

Adequate exposure is often a point of confusion:

- You will not be forgiven for inadequately exposing a relevant area of the body and therefore missing a physical sign.

- You will be frowned upon for unnecessarily exposing an area and therefore potentially embarrassing a patient.

- In male patients there is not normally an issue about embarrassment through exposure of the chest wall.

- In female patients, when exposing the chest wall be sensitive and polite. It is generally better to expose the chest for as little time as possible, ie just before you examine the chest wall rather than right from the beginning.

- If in doubt in your finals exam it is probably better to err on the side of over- rather than under-exposure of a patient. In an example case of neurofibromatosis where the only signs are on the chest wall, you will probably fail the station if you do not expose the top half of the patient and therefore miss the diagnosis. Compare this to a case where you thought there could be signs on the chest wall, you asked politely and sensitively if you could inspect the chest wall, but did not see any findings. In this example, as long as you can justify why you thought it necessary to inspect the chest wall, neither the patient not the examiner is likely to get upset.

> Adequate exposure is vital for a good examination of the relevant body system or area. Think through all of your examinations beforehand to work out how much exposure each requires and when.

Observation

Observation of the patient begins as soon as you enter the room. End of the bed inspection should actually be from the end of the bed. As in a driving test, you should be seen to perform particular aspects of the examination or the examiner will assume they have not been done. A good way to do this is to first introduce yourself to the patient, stating that you are going to have a quick look from the end of the bed, and then going to stand at the foot of the bed. Sweep your gaze around the room and then focus on the patient. Be aware of how uncomfortable it feels for the patient to be stared at, and try to move your gaze rapidly but systematically down the patient.

Observation for items around the bed should include:

- boxes of tablets;

- inhalers;

- infusions;

- oxygen – rate and type of administration;

- walking aids to suggest limited exercise tolerance;

- signs such as 'fluid restrict 1 litre', 'low protein diet';

- chest drain bottles.

When observing the patient pay particular attention to:

- approximate age;

- ethnicity;

- colour, ie pallor, flushing, cyanosis and jaundice;

- comfort, ie in respiratory distress or pain;

- striking physical characteristics suggestive of a syndrome, for example marfanoid appearance;

- cachexia;

- scars on chest, abdomen and limbs;

- lines.

> A large amount of information can be gleaned from the end of the bed, and you should never rush this part of the examination.

Presenting your findings

It is a good idea as part of your preparation to practise providing a commentary while examining a patient. You should assume that the examiners would prefer that you carry out your examination, and then formally present your findings at the end. However, if short of time or faced with a patient with a few particularly interesting signs that the examiners wish to demonstrate, they may break down the examination into stages and ask you to describe your findings as they appear.

Talk through:

- Advantage – you can explain and describe your findings as you find them, therefore reducing the likelihood of you forgetting them at the end.

- Disadvantage – unless you practise this style, then talking as you examine is likely to slow you down and you may distract yourself and forget how to perform a slick examination.

Presenting at the end:

- Advantage – you can put together the findings while performing the last parts of the examination, come to a list of differentials and think of a management plan.

- Disadvantage – rapid thought is required to summarize your findings and come to differentials, and unless you practise this you may end up losing your way or coming across as very unsure of your findings when trying to summarize under the harsh gaze of the examiners.

For more advice on how to present your OSCE findings, see Chapter 9, 'Active answering'.

Making up findings

There is a lot of pressure as soon as you enter each OSCE station to pick up a wealth of clinical signs. As you introduce yourself to the patient your mind is already running through the top five or 10 most common exam cases for this station. What happens if you are unable to pick up a primary diagnosis? In this hypothetical situation you find several peripheral stigmata of a disease, but are unable to identify the murmur, or the pleural effusion, or the ascites or hepatomegaly that you were hoping to find. You have several options:

Re-examination of the relevant part. This is far from ideal as it alerts the examiner that, having finished an otherwise thorough and slick examination routine, you missed key signs and have to return, ie your examination skills are poor and you don't recognize signs when you find them. From the moment you signal, either verbally or through your actions, that you are re-examining an area, the examiner will be considering if you are a pass/fail candidate. It is entirely reasonable, despite you apologizing to them and the patient for having to 'quickly re-examine the posterior chest', that they refuse your request and force you to present your findings.

Having said this, if you truly feel that the risks are worth taking, then politely apologize to the patient that you would like to quickly re-examine a particular area, and then confidently and rapidly do so. If you are lucky, the examiner may not realize, or may let you continue but will expect an excellent presentation of your findings.

If you routinely find yourself leaving out parts of the examination, consider whether you should slow down your routine, or whether other types of practice would be beneficial (see Chapter 7, 'Simulations').

Present what you have found. This is also suboptimal as you only have a patchy collection of signs, and aren't really sure about the diagnosis. It is important to start off strongly with the findings that you have identified. Include all the important negatives such as 'no stigmata of infective endocarditis' so that the examiner understands that you have been observant and have made a thorough clinical examination. If we use a case of right-sided consolidation as our example, and you noted slightly decreased chest expansion on the right with a dull percussion note, could hear air entry throughout the right chest but no bronchial breathing or whispering pectoriloquy, you should present the case as a probable right consolidation with differentials including a pleural effusion.

In this setting it is vital to state why you are unsure (perhaps the examiners agree with you – they will have examined the patient that morning), and what you would like to do to further elucidate the diagnosis, for example requesting a chest radiograph.

Make up a finding that you think ought to be present. This is generally acknowledged to be the fastest route to a fail. The commonest reason for not being able to identify an expected sign is that it just isn't there – the examiners are not always able to find 'classic' cases. The patient in your OSCE may have splinter haemorrhages, Oslers' nodes, Janeway lesions, a murmur and a fever, but have no clubbing or splenomegaly. Making up physical signs is definitely not advised and if found out (usually quite quickly), the examiners will then doubt everything you say from then on.

Never, ever make up a physical sign that you didn't actually identify.

General tips

You should aim to carry out a swift but thorough examination in an orthodox manner.

You must always warn the patient and briefly explain any parts of the examination which are slightly more intimate; for example:

- Palpation of the apex beat – 'Would it be okay if I felt for your heartbeat?'

- Palpation of chest expansion – 'I would like to place my hands on your chest to assess how much each side moves.'

If you are seen to cause the patient pain or distress you will generally be looking at a swift fail, so always ask the patient right at the start if they are in pain and if they are happy with you examining them.

Don't forget that the cases are pretty much all stable chronic conditions and the patients well enough to be examined for the entire day, ie ruling out most acute conditions such as pneumonia or heart failure unless they happen to be stable after their initial treatment and the examiners are getting desperate for cases.

Be prepared to perform any 'extra test' that you request or mention, for example using a Snellen chart, jaw jerk reflex, corneal sensation and feeling for peripheral pulses.

Listen carefully for any clues in your instructions as to the patient's condition. For example you may be told that they presented with chest pain, fever or breathlessness.

Below are the main examinations with notes on particular aspects commonly missed or poorly performed.

Cardiology

Common cases:

1 Prosthetic valves – Are there features of infective endocarditis, over-warfarinization or valve failure?

2 AS, MR, mixed valvular disease (eg AS and MR, or AS and AR) – How severe is the lesion? In mixed valvular disease, which is the predominant lesion?

3 AF – commonly in association with mitral stenosis/regurgitation. Look for features of an old CVA or over-warfarinization.

4 HOCM – Remember to ask for an ECHO to confirm your findings.

5 Marfan's syndrome – often associated with AR or mitral valve prolapse.

- Introduce yourself, gain consent, ask about any painful areas, position at 45°.
- Around the bed:
    - GTN spray, infusion pumps, oxygen therapy;
    - Walking stick, wheelchair.
- End of the bed:
    - Metallic heart sound;
    - Scars on chest and legs.
- Hands:
    - spending any more than about five seconds is probably too long, and you should practise scanning rapidly for the peripheral stigmata of subacute bacterial endocarditis.
- Pulse:
    - Radial pulse – take your time to confirm or exclude rate-controlled atrial fibrillation. Work out the rate exactly by either timing over 10 or 15 seconds and multiplying by six or four appropriately. The presence of AF may signify the presence of mitral stenosis, so be alert for a mid-diastolic murmur.
    - Radioradial delay.
    - Ask for a blood pressure after taking a pulse – may give a big clue for valve lesions of aortic stenosis or aortic regurgitation.
    - Collapsing pulse – several well-described ways of performing this test, but the main points are:

— Check again with the patient for pain, especially shoulder injuries;

— Look like you have done it hundreds of times before;

— Know what you are feeling for – a 'tapping' quality of the radial pulse against your palm or fingers.

- Pulse, JVP, face:

  – A rapid method of examining the JVP is to confirm a position of approximately 45°, ask the patient to look to the left, and then look at their right ear lobe to spot movement caused by a grossly elevated JVP. If this is not present, slowly move your gaze down towards the head of the clavicle. If you are still unable to see the JVP it is either above the level of the earlobe or below the level of the clavicle. Therefore first place the back of your finger at the base of the JVP just above the head of the clavicle to obstruct venous return to see if the vein distends, and secondly try to elicit the hepatojugular reflux.

  – *Listen* for the clicking of a metallic valve, especially while examining the JVP, central pulse and face.

  – Comment on dentition (source of septic emboli for SBE).

- Palpation:

  – Note whether the apex beat is displaced, as, if present, it tells you there is volume overload in the left ventricle due to a regurgitant murmur into the left ventricle such as mitral or aortic regurgitation.

  – What is the character of the beat?

    — Can you confidently and consistently differentiate between a heave, lift, tap and thrill?

    — One way around this is to characterize the valve lesion through assessment of the pulse and auscultation, and then to retrospectively label the apex beat character with the appropriate description, eg LV heave and aortic thrill associated with aortic stenosis.

    — Another solution is to merely comment on whether the apex beat is displaced, and secondly if it is 'forceful'.

Don't get so focused on labelling the nature of the apex beat that you forget the other many key points which help you to characterize which valve lesion is present.

- Auscultation:
  - Palpate a central pulse (either subclavian or carotid) while auscultating at the apex to tune yourself into the first and second heart sounds, but never use your thumb to feel a carotid pulse, and let go of the central pulse once you have oriented yourself – otherwise it will be uncomfortable for the patient.
  - Don't forget the manoeuvres and breath holds – a standard examination would include:
    — left lateral position using the bell of the stethoscope for MR;
    — sitting forward in expiration listening at the left lower sternal edge for AR;
    — carotids for bruits/radiation of AS;
    — left axilla for radiation of MR.

- It is acceptable to percuss and auscultate only the lung bases to assess for pulmonary oedema.

- Inspect and palpate the lower limbs:
  - Calf – vein harvest scars;
  - Ankles – pitting oedema, note how far up it extends.

- 'To complete the examination I would like to...'
  - BP (if you haven't already asked for it, although we would advise you to ask for it after taking the pulse, as it could be pathognomonic for certain valvular lesions);
  - urine dipstick;
  - fundoscopy;
  - temperature.

PITFALLS

- Presenting your findings, avoiding common mistakes:
  - Introductory sentence: 'This patient was comfortable at rest with a GTN spray on his table. He had a midline sternotomy scar and a vein harvest scar on his left calf.'
  - Give an exact number for the pulse, ie not 'approximately', or 'roughly', or 'about' 80 beats per minute.
  - If you are very confident in your diagnosis, then a distinction answer could take the form of a diagnosis with a qualified explanation; for example: 'This patient has aortic stenosis as evidenced by a slow rising pulse with a low systolic blood pressure and an ejection systolic murmur heard loudest at the aortic region and radiating up to the carotids. I would like to further characterize the lesion though echocardiography.'

- If you are slightly less confident, then you can always describe your findings, but be aware of the potential of boring your examiners; so group findings together and summarize relevant areas; for example: 'This patient had no peripheral stigmata of infective endocarditis. There was a slow rising pulse and a low blood pressure. The JVP was not elevated. The apex beat was not displaced. There was an ejection systolic murmur heard loudest at the aortic region and which radiated up to the carotids.'

- Note that in this latter example by the time you come to giving a diagnosis you have 70% of the marks, so even if you get the wrong diagnosis, as long as you describe how you investigate further, you should probably pass. The first example has a higher margin for error, but if correct looks much more slick.

- Two murmurs:

  - Just because you have identified a murmur you should not relax – your task has just started. Continue to listen for other murmurs, and start thinking about the features of the valve lesion you are suspecting.

  - It is common for patients to have mixed valvular disease, so if you think there is a pansystolic murmur audible at the apex radiating to the axilla and also a soft ejection systolic murmur loudest at the aortic region, then you should present these findings, stating that you would like an echocardiogram to confirm your suspicions.

  - Aortic stenosis? Is there coexistent aortic regurgitation?

  - You should ideally state which valve lesion you think is dominant – often very difficult, but as long as you qualify your answer and state that you would like to follow up with an echocardiogram the examiners will give you credit.

- Key points if a valve lesion is suspected:

  - Severity:

    — AS – slow rising pulse, soft S2, reversed splitting;

    — AR – collapsing pulse, hyperdynamic apex beat, presence of several eponymous signs; for example Corrigan's, Quincke's and Duroziez's signs;

    — MR – displaced apex beat caused by dilatation of the left ventricle;

    — MS – prolonged diastolic murmur.

  - Associated findings:

    — Atrial fibrillation;

    — Mitral facies.

- Important points if a prosthetic valve is suspected:

  - Signs of over-anticoagulation;

  - Signs of infective endocarditis;

  - Signs of valve failure, eg regurgitation, associated with heart failure.

Never ever make up a finding because you expected to find it. The examiners will have examined the patient that morning and will know which signs are present. If they suspect you are 'creating' physical signs they will soon fail you.

Respiratory

Common cases:

1 Pneumonectomy/lobectomy – look for differentials of the common underlying conditions that might require a pneumonectomy such as bronchiectasis, non small cell bronchial carcinoma and old cases of TB.

2 Pulmonary fibrosis – think of the differentials of upper versus lower zone fibrosis.

3 Bronchiectasis – are there features to suggest cystic fibrosis, bronchial carcinoma or Marfans disease?

4 Pleural effusion – think of the common causes of exudates and transudates.

5 COPD – are there features of right heart failure, active infection or side effects of steroid use?

● Introduce yourself, gain consent, ask about any painful areas, position in a comfortable seated position.

● Around the bed:
  – Oxygen therapy – which type and concentration? Note if they are on two litres of nasal oxygen, ie likely they are on long-term oxygen therapy and suffer from COPD.
  – Inhalers – Do they suffer from asthma or COPD? Look for the giveaway round inhaler of tiotropium.
  – Sputum pot – If you find one, then it's there for a reason and you should definitely open it and examine the sputum, noting colour and the presence of blood.
  – Peak flow meter – Don't forget to use this at the end of the examination to check their peak flow.

● End of the bed:
  – Comfort – breathless or comfortable?
  – Nutritional state – note if the patient is markedly cachectic.

- Colour – 'blue bloater or pink puffer'?
- Work of breathing – accessory muscles, tracheal tug, intercostal and subcostal recession.
- Added noises – audible wheeze, prolonged expiratory phase.
- Scars – lobectomy or pneumonectomy?
- Face – look for ptosis, meiosis, enophthalmos and anhydrosis of Horner's syndrome.

- Hands:
  - Tar staining.
  - Intrinsic muscle wasting – a clue that may indicate a Pancoast tumour.
  - Cyanosis.
  - Nail bed pallor;
  - CO_2 retention flap – Ask the patient to hold their arms outstretched with wrists extended for five to 10 seconds in order to elicit asterixis.

- Pulse and respiratory rate:
  - It is perfectly acceptable to count the respiratory rate after counting the pulse, and one method is to count the pulse over 15 seconds and then while keeping your hand on the radial pulse, change your gaze to the chest wall and count the number of breaths over the next 15 seconds.
  - Also reasonable is to count the respiratory rate while performing the inspection from the end of the bed.

- Palpation of lymph nodes:
  - It is acceptable to palpate for cervical nodes from the front of the patient in a respiratory examination, or you could wait until the patient sits forward and palpate them from behind before examining the posterior chest wall.
  - Whichever method you use, the key is to be rapid – you are performing a 'screen' of cervical lymphadenopathy and, as such, should take no more than a few seconds.

- Chest:
  - Inspection:
    — Take care to look laterally and raise the patient's arms in order not to miss old axillary scars.
    — Your first clue of asymmetrical expansion will be found here.

- Palpation:
    - Expansion should be assessed rapidly and confidently by placing your hands on the anterior upper chest wall and in the submammary area. Posteriorly it is acceptable to assess expansion at only one area which is towards the bases.
    - Either tactile vocal fremitus or vocal resonance should be performed, but it is not necessary to perform both. In each case ask the patient to repeat the words 'ninety nine' while either palpating the relevant zone with the ulnar border of the hand, or auscultating with your stethoscope.
- Percussion:
    - Each area should be percussed with two strikes and no more.
    - Unless the patient is exceptionally tall you should be percussing in six areas anteriorly (starting above the clavicles), one in each axilla and six posteriorly.
    - You should resist the temptation to pause your examination to percuss at great length an area which has significant findings such as dullness at the left base. Spending great lengths at a particular area or returning to it at the end looks amateurish and hesitant.
- Auscultation:
    - Only listen for the duration of one breath sound in each area.
    - As a rough guide you should listen in the same places you percussed, ie six anteriorly, one in each axilla, and six posteriorly.
- Note that the reason why you should practise limiting yourself to percussing twice and listening for only one breath in each area is not only to decrease the total time of the examination, but also because many examiners think it unnecessary to repeatedly percuss or listen to an area, arguing that with practice you should know what bronchial breathing sounds like and therefore if you heard it, there is no need to listen at greater length to confirm the finding.
- 'To complete the examination I would like to...'
    - measure the peak flow;
    - get a temperature;
    - measure the oxygen saturations;
    - look at the sputum pot.

PITFALLS

- Random diagnosis given in panic:

  - Students often find it difficult to put together the findings of a respiratory examination. In the heat of the moment the pressure of presenting and the numerous signs identified can sometimes result in a panic, with the examiner being surprised by a fairly random and 'snatched' diagnosis, having been presented with a good set of clinical signs.

  - The answer is to do several things:

    — Practise, practise, practise – and not just any practice, but thoughtful, considered practice where you examine a patient while a colleague looks on (playing the part of the examiner, and critiquing later). After you leave the bedside go to a nearby quiet area and present your findings formally to your colleague, or, even better, to a senior doctor.

    — Run through the examination steps, imagining each stage in detail, and doing it in turn for each of the major clinical scenarios; for example, pneumothorax, pleural effusion, fibrosis, consolidation and lobectomy or pneumonectomy.

    — Write down the distinguishing examination findings of the main respiratory diagnoses so that the moment you find one of them, you are starting to focus your mind towards a particular diagnosis. For example, once you have identified a dull percussion note you are trying to distinguish between a pleural effusion and consolidation, and because you are already focused in on those two diagnoses, the finding of either bronchial breathing and vocal resonance or markedly reduced breath sounds will rapidly lead you to a diagnosis.

- Hyper-resonant percussion note on one side or is it a dull percussion note on the other?

  - Practise, practise, practise – the art of percussion is not solely in the audible note, but also in the tactile feedback from the finger placed on the chest wall. After a while you should be able to tell that not only does the percussion of a pleural effusion lead to a 'dull' sound, but also produces very little 'give' on the percussed finger.

  - It is extremely unlikely that a patient with a pneumothorax large enough to produce clinical signs is presented in an examination without being drained first. Therefore the odds are that a differential percussion note is explained by collapse, consolidation or effusion, ie the abnormal side is the 'dull' side.

- Testing for expansion:

  - Examiners often remark that testing for expansion is performed poorly. The most likely explanation is that it is a stage of the examination which is neglected up until a few weeks before the exam, most students leaving this aspect of the examination out while examining patients on the wards as they are concerned it may cause embarrassment to themselves or the patient.

- It is vital to be confident but not insensitive, as this is a vital aspect of assessing for asymmetrical chest movement but is fairly intimate in nature.

- As with any such examination, warn the patient, explaining what you would like to do and why. For example: 'I would like to check the movement of your chest by placing my hands around your chest. Would that be all right?'

The respiratory examination is very commonly performed but because students rarely practise the full examination they are not used to integrating the many physical signs into a unifying diagnosis.

Gastrointestinal

Common cases:

1 Chronic liver disease – look for signs to suggest a cause, and for common complications such as splenomegaly resulting from portal hypertension, encephalopathy, bruising, and ascites.

2 Hepatomegaly, splenomegaly, hepatosplenomegaly – look for clues to suggest myeloproliferative disorders such as bruising, pallor and sepsis. Look for lymphadenopathy, which may suggest an underlying lymphoproliferative disorder, and for signs of chronic liver disease.

3 Ascites – look for signs of right heart failure, a low protein state and intra-abdominal malignancy.

4 Transplanted kidney – you should try to comment on the underlying cause that led to transplantation, on signs of previous dialysis such as AV fistulae and scars of CAPD, and on the presence of side effects of immunosuppression.

5 Abdominal mass, lymphadenopathy – look carefully for subtle scars, and think of the differentials for a mass in that region.

● Introduce yourself, gain consent, ask about any painful areas, position supine with hands by their sides and head on one pillow.

- Around the bed:
  - Signs giving clues to the underlying condition; for example, low-protein diet or fluid restriction;
  - Infusions or PCA pump.

- End of the bed inspection:
  - Colour – jaundice, pallor, pigmentation (haemochromatosis).
  - Bruising to suggest coagulopathy and liver failure.
  - Nutritional state – note the presence of cachexia.
  - Abdominal distension and localized masses – you are unlikely to be able to pick up an abdominal mass on inspection, but should appreciate if there is generalized distension.
  - Scars, especially from liver or kidney transplant.
  - Side effects of immunosuppressives:
    - Cyclosporine – tremor, gum hypertrophy, excessive hair growth.
    - Tacrolimus – tremor, itchy rash (look for excoriation marks).
    - Azathioprine – hair loss, itchy rash (look for excoriation marks).
    - Mycophenylate – tremor.
    - Note: all of the above cause bone marrow suppression and therefore thrombocytopenia (petechial bruising), anaemia (pallor) and neutropenia (opportunistic infections).
    - Prednisolone – Cushingoid appearance.

Central lines and dialysis catheters:

- Central venous catheter – internal jugular and femoral:
  - pro: relatively easy and quick to insert, enabling monitoring of central pressures;
  - con: high risk of line sepsis, so removed after approximately 5–7 days.
- Dialysis catheters – non-tunnelled and tunnelled:
  - pro: lower infection rates;
  - con: more difficult and time consuming to insert.
- Peritoneal dialysis catheter – Tenchkoff is the most commonly used.
- Look for evidence of line sepsis – erythematous skin or pus.

- Hands:
  - Nail changes – koilonychias, leukonychia, pallor;
  - Palms – pallor, palmar erythema, Dupuytren's contracture;
  - Asterixis – tested in the same way as described in the respiratory section;
  - Diabetic blood sugar testing marks.

- Arms:
  - Arteriovenous fistulas – look for old fistulas, and then when you find a working fistula note if there are any signs of local sepsis. Be extremely gentle and ask specific permission from the patient to feel for a thrill or auscultate for a bruit.

- Sclerae, face and chest:
  - Jaundice;
  - Signs of chronic liver disease including parotid swelling, gynaecomastia and spider naevi.

- Abdomen:
  - Inspection:
    — Caput medusae – practise differentiating between these and collateral veins secondary to IVC obstruction. Test direction of flow in veins *below* the umbilicus – caput medusae will refill with flow towards the legs, and collateral veins from IVC obstruction will refill towards the head.
    — Don't forget to look at the flanks, loin and groin for the J-shaped (hockey stick-shaped) renal transplant scars.
    — Note any divarification of the recti as the patient shifts position.
    — If a scar site looks new, note discharge/erythema around the wound.
    — Look carefully for laparoscopic surgery porthole sites.
  - Palpation:
    — From the moment palpation starts you should have your hand and elbow at the same level as the abdomen, which for most people translates into kneeling on the floor. The argument is that only when the wrist is in a neutral position can adequate flexion and extension and therefore palpation be achieved.
    — A standard examination divides the abdomen into nine sections and starts in the left iliac fossa unless the patient tells you that there is a particularly painful area, in which case you palpate that section last.
    — Light palpation to 'screen' for any masses or tender areas.
    — Deep palpation to further elucidate the nature of any mass.

— Ballot the kidneys.

— Feel for inguinal herniae.

- Special tests:

  — Palpation for hepatomegaly.

  — Begin in the right iliac fossa.

  — Commonly performed badly; practise the pattern of palpation for a liver edge during inspiration when the liver is most inferior, and then shifting your hand position on expiration.

  — If you feel a liver edge you should note: size (centimetres or fingerbreadths below the costal margin); tenderness – more suggestive of hepatitis; firmness – hard suggests malignancy; texture – smooth or 'nobbly'.

  — Percuss out the margins:

    — Map out both the inferior and superior margins by tapping from resonant to dull, starting in the right iliac fossa and also from the right anterior chest wall.

  — Palpation for splenomegaly:
    — Begin in the right iliac fossa.
    — The pattern is the same as that used to detect hepatomegaly.
    — If you feel an enlarged spleen you should be able to differentiate it from a renal mass and therefore note that for splenomegaly: unable to get above it; notched; moves with respiration; dull to percussion; also note the size in either centimetres or fingerbreadths below the left costal margin.

  — Shifting dullness test for ascites:
    — Often performed badly, it is important as a screening tool for patients with liver failure if suspecting ascites.
    — The theory is that fluid will settle to the most dependent part of the abdomen when the patient is rolled, hence a dull percussion note caused by fluid in the flanks will become resonant once that fluid is shifted.
    — Percuss at the level of the umbilicus from the midline towards the patient's left flank. When you encounter dullness spread your fingers such that the middle finger is on the transitional point, your index is over the resonant area and your ring finger is over the dull area (confirm by percussing on each finger).
    — Ask the patient to roll 45° to their right (towards you), while keeping your hand in the same position on the abdomen, wait a few seconds and then re-percuss.
    — A positive shifting dullness sign should show that on percussion of your ring finger which previously had a dull note, there is now a resonant note.

Practise examining for enlarged livers, spleens and for ascites, as it is difficult to identify the many characteristics of an enlarged organ in the brief time you are allowed during an OSCE.

- Auscultation:
    - Bowel sounds – it doesn't matter where you place your stethoscope for this.
    - Bruits over the aorta and renal arteries.
- 'To complete the examination I would like to...'
    - examine the external genitalia;
    - perform a digital rectal examination;
    - dipstick the urine;
    - check the temperature.

KEY POINT

You *must* take the time to go to a transplant ward to learn about different scars, post-op complications and side effects of long-term immunosuppressant use. Try to get an idea of the frequency of underlying conditions causing renal and hepatic failure.

Neurology

Common cases:

1 Peripheral neuropathy – look for signs of diabetic finger testing, cachexia and clubbing to suggest carcinoma, and scars to suggest transplantation and long-term immunosuppressive use.

2 Hemiplegia – look for clues to suggest thrombosis, embolus or haemorrhage as a cause. Think of the territory affected and its blood supply. Consider PFO, hypercoagulable states and polycystic kidney disease in the young patient.

3 Motor neurone disease – is it predominantly amyotrophic lateral sclerosis, progressive muscular atrophy or progressive bulbar palsy?

4 Cerebellar syndrome – ask to perform a full cranial nerve examination to look for signs of multiple sclerosis, and a cardiovascular examination to look for signs of valvular or carotid disease.

5 Ulnar, median, radial nerve palsy – look for signs of likely causes such as proximal fractures or arthritis. State that you would like to ask the patient their occupation and to examine for other nerves which are involved.

Examiners love to test students on neurology stations as they feel that above all others, this is the examination that students practise least. They are absolutely correct in this assumption and you should guard against it by taking extra care to practise your examination technique and interpretation of physical signs.

Introduce yourself, gain consent, ask if there are any painful areas and position the patient appropriately. For example, when asked to examine the cranial nerves the patient should be sat upright on a chair or on the side of the bed. When performing an upper limb peripheral nerve examination, the patient should be positioned semi-recumbent on a couch, and supine with their head on one pillow for a lower limb peripheral nerve examination.

Cranial nerve examination

This is actually a great opportunity to show the examiner a slick, professional examination.

Acceptable strategies include either proceeding strictly numerically from cranial nerve I to XII or to group several nerves together. For example, while testing the facial nerve and asking the patient to show their teeth, you could ask them to open their mouth against resistance (V), say 'Ahhh' (IX and X) and stick their tongue out and move it from side to side (XII).

The main point is to find a way that is not too unorthodox and works smoothly for you, and then practise and practise until it becomes second nature.

It is polite and sensitive to say thank you after each request, otherwise the overall impression is of a doctor barking out commands of an embarrassing nature to a patient who is suffering from a neurological condition but who has been kind enough to give their time to help with examinations.

Your examiner will be more lenient should you make a mistake if you have shown sensitivity and politeness while examining the patient.

The following section outlines the main points in the testing of each nerve, and also provides an example instruction to ask the patient to perform each test.

- End of the bed inspection:
    - Asymmetry – unilateral facial droop;
    - Eyes – ptosis, false eye, dilated pupil, deviated gaze and nystagmus at rest;
    - Ears – hearing aid;
    - Features of Parkinsonism – expressionless, masklike, oily skin, decreased blink rate, slow movements;
    - Involuntary movements.
- I: Acceptable to merely ask about any changes: 'Have you noticed any change in your sense of smell?'
- II: Several aspects to this examination; think pupils, fields, acuity, fundi. Note that pupils are actually controlled by the occulomotor nerve (III) but it is acceptable and easier to examine them while examining the optic nerve.
    - Pupils:
        - Do direct and consensual light reflexes while placing your hand in the midline to prevent the light source cross-contaminating the other eye: 'I am going to shine a light in your eyes.'
    - Be seen to be looking for both the direct and consensual reflexes, ie shine a light in the left eye while looking at the left eye for the direct reflex, and then shine a light again in the left eye while looking in their right for the consensual reflex.
    - Also perform the swinging flashlight test, looking for a relative afferent pupillary defect.
- Accommodation:
    - 'Please look at my finger and follow it in from a distance.'
- Visual fields:
    - There are several methods; find a way that is rapid and reliable. The confrontation method is widely used and described below.
    - Ensure you are seated approximately one metre away and at the same eye level.
    - Ask the patient to start with their left eye by covering their right eye with their right hand. Ensure the patient is looking directly at your right eye.

- Cover your left eye with your left hand while testing the temporal fields with the right hand, and then swap and cover your left eye with your right hand, now using your left hand to test the nasal fields.

- When your free hand is placed at the limits of peripheral gaze such that you can see your finger with your peripheral vision, move your finger to test whether they can identify when it moves.

- While this sounds complicated, it is easy to do and ensures that your arm is always outside the visual field and therefore does not shield your moving fingers. Your instructions should be clear and precise, with phrases such as: 'Please cover your right eye with your right hand and look straight at my eye;' 'When you see my finger move, say yes.' Note that the patient can keep the same hand covering the left eye even though you will need to swap halfway.

- To conclude, you should state your intention to test acuity and examine the fundi: 'I would like to test acuity with a Snellen chart;' 'I would like to perform fundoscopy.'

- III, IV, VI: Pupillary movements:

  - You are testing the action of the external ocular muscles, and as such an H shape with or without a vertical midline addition is standard: 'Please keep your head still, follow my finger with your eyes and tell me if you see double.'

  - The instruction given has three distinct parts, each of which is absolutely vital to prevent misunderstanding, typically manifested by the patient turning their head to follow your finger, not following your finger with their gaze, or not telling you when they see double.

- V: Remember to test both motor and sensory functions:

  - To test sensation, use light touch on both sides in branches a, b and c.

  - It is not necessary to get the patient to close their eyes but you must ask them to tell you if it feels different on the right compared to the left: 'I am going to touch your face. Please tell me if it feels the same on both sides.'

  - To test motor function, you can assess mouth opening against resistance (lateral pterygoid muscles): 'Please open your mouth and resist me closing it.'

  - The other test of motor function is to assess contraction of the masseter and temporal muscles: 'Please clench your teeth' (simultaneously feel over the temporalis for muscle contraction).

- VII: One of the most visible lesions from the end of the bed, yet so easily missed in the heat of the moment. Make sure you look carefully for facial asymmetry at rest before giving any instructions.

  - There are several different commands to select from and it is not necessary to use all of them.

- You are testing for gross right versus left defects and upper versus lower motor neuron deficits: 'Please raise your eyebrows;' 'Please screw up your eyes tightly;' 'Please show me your teeth.'
  - If you spot a facial droop you must work out if it results from an upper or a lower motor neuron lesion by seeing if there is forehead sparing (the forehead has bilateral upper motor neurone innervation and so is preserved in an upper motor neurone lesion).

- VIII: Again, remember this is testing for gross defects, so standard options are:
  - Rubbing your fingers beside the patient's ear: 'Please tell me which side you can hear a noise.'
  - Whispering a number in one ear while occluding the other: 'I am going to whisper a number in your ear; please tell me what it is.'

- IX, X: The first indication of a lesion may be a hoarse voice or bovine cough.

- You are looking for deviation of the uvula when the palate is elevated through phonation: 'Please open your mouth wide and say Ahhh.'

- XI: Test trapezius: 'Please shrug your shoulders and push against me.'

- Test sternocleidomastoid, noting that when the patient turns their head to the left against resistance, it is the right sternocleidomastoid and therefore right accessory nerve being tested: 'Please turn your head to the left and push against my hand.'

- XII: You are looking for gross wasting or fasciculations, deviation of the tongue when it is protruded in the midline, and for abnormal movement on side-to-side testing: 'Please can you stick your tongue out straight in the middle;' 'Please can you move it from side to side.'

- Note that while the above examination is listed in order of ascending cranial nerves, a more slick version would be to group them as follows:
  - I
  - II
  - III, IV, VI
  - V (sensory)
  - VII, V (motor), IX, X, XII
  - VIII
  - XI.

> The cranial nerve examination requires the patient to perform several uncomfortable and embarrassing tasks so, phrase your instructions politely and sensitively.

- It is important to be clear which 'special tests' you would like to mention while you are examining the cranial nerves, and which you would like to mention at the end. The list shown below assumes that no tests were mentioned during the examination:
  - 'To complete my examination I would like to...'
    - perform fundoscopy;
    - test acuity with a Snellen chart;
    - assess the blind spot;
    - test the corneal reflex;
    - assess the jaw jerk;
    - conduct Rinne and Weber's tests;
    - examine for cerebellar signs' (only if suggested by the presence of ataxia, nystagmus, tremor, slurred speech, internuclear opthalmoplegia or enlarged blindspot).

- Note that the above are best presented in order of I to XII.

- As long as you have a consistent and easily memorable method it doesn't matter which special tests you choose to mention during the examination and which you want to list at the end.

- Tests you are not expected to mention are:
  - Formal olfactory testing;
  - Formal visual field testing;
  - Formal auditory testing;
  - Checking colour vision.

PITFALLS

- Poor testing of visual fields:
  - Unnecessarily complex or inadequately precise instructions.
  - Remember that you are merely performing a quick screening for gross field defects, hence the waggling finger method is acceptable.
  - You can also move the waggling' finger in from the periphery and ask the patient to say yes when they see it, rather than when they see your finger move when it is placed just inside the visual field. The problem with this method is that sometimes patients misinterpret movement of your arm as being able to see your waggling finger, hence it is more robust to use the method described above.

- Testing eye movements:
  - Students often accidently test extremes of gaze and therefore elicit (perfectly normal) nystagmus at the limits of lateral gaze.
  - Practise on colleagues to realize that you do not need to move your hand far from the midline in order to test lateral gaze.
- Try to resist the temptation of performing the action you are asking of the patient as it looks unprofessional to stick your tongue out at the patient or to bare your teeth at them. The only exception is if the patient truly fails to understand your instructions, but once again it is probably because your instruction is not concise or clear.
- Getting deviations of the uvula and tongue mixed up when testing the IX/X and XII nerves:
  - The uvula is *pulled* up and therefore towards the normal side, ie deviates *away* from the lesion.
  - The tongue is *pushed* out and therefore away from the normal side, ie deviates *towards* the lesion.

Practise the list of verbal instructions you will give to the patient so that even when under the stress of the exam you will appear competent and composed.

Peripheral nerve examination:

- Examiners pride themselves on being able to spot weaker candidates by the way they use a tendon hammer. A few simple tips:
  - Always hold it near the pointed end.
  - Practise swinging it gently with a relaxed wrist so you don't produce too much force and hurt the patient.
  - All reflexes must be elicited from the patient's right side.
  - It is standard practice to place your left index finger over the tendon when testing the bicep and supinator reflexes in order to minimize patient discomfort.
  - Know how to perform reinforcement for those patients who find it difficult to relax – jaw clenching for upper limb reflexes and the Jendrassik manoeuvre for lower limb reflexes.
  - You must practise on patients and friends until you can reliably elicit each reflex with only one strike of the tendon hammer.

- Due to the large range of movements involved it is extremely important to ask the patient if there are any painful joints or muscles before you start.

- It is orthodox to proceed in the general order of tone, power, reflexes, sensation and coordination but some variation is acceptable as long as the examination is swift and assured.

- Learn the pattern of different findings for an upper versus a lower motor neurone lesion:
  - UMN:
    — Inspection – fasciculations, no atrophy (or only slight, from disuse);
    — Tone – increased (spastic), with clonus;
    — Power – weak;
    — Reflexes – hyper-reflexic.
  - LMN:
    — Inspection – wasting, no fasciculations;
    — Tone – decreased (floppy);
    — Power – weak;
    — Reflexes – absent/decreased.

- You are unusually fortunate in having the possibility of a 'normal' side to use as a comparison, so make sure you test everything in steps, comparing left with right. This will enable you to pick up subtle relative differences especially in tone, power, reflexes and sensation.

- When testing power you should always aim to overcome the effort of the patient otherwise you may miss more subtle degrees of weakness.

Upper limb examination:

- Around the bed inspection:
  - Walking aids, wheelchair.

- End of the bed inspection:
  - Don't neglect the face for clues (see cranial nerve examination).
  - Unusual posture, deformity.
  - Tremor.
  - Muscle wasting.

- Tone:
  - It is important to ensure the patient is as relaxed as possible.
  - Gently rotate the shoulder.
  - Flex and extend the elbow at different speeds to elicit leadpipe rigidity and prevent the patient from guessing the action you are about to perform and add voluntary movements.
  - Two distinct movements should be performed at the wrist – rotation and flexion/extension to elicit cogwheel rigidity.
- Power:
  - Learn the MRC grading system and myotomes.
  - Each muscle tested should be mentally noted in terms of the above.
  - Test each muscle group; mentally you should be able to account for the function of roots C5 to T1:
    - Shoulder abduction/adduction.
    - Elbow flexion/extension.
    - Wrist flexion/extension.
    - Finger abduction and power grip.
    - Understand the difference between testing myotomes and individual nerve function, ie median nerve testing would involve thumb abduction but is not necessary in a standard upper limb neurological examination.
    - You are carrying out a screening examination, and any lesions identified can later be examined in greater detail.
- Reflexes:
  - Be proficient in testing the biceps, triceps and supinator limb jerks.
  - If you are not able to elicit a particular reflex, initially do your best to get the patient to relax, and if that is not successful then ask the patient to clench their teeth.
  - If despite all the above you are not able to elicit a reflex and you feel you have given two or three good attempts, then do not persist and cause the patient any further discomfort. It may be possible that there is a perfectly good reason for a lack of reflex on that side.
- Coordination:
  - Finger–nose testing for dysmetria and tremor.
  - Dysdiadochokinesis.

- Pronator drift – Ask the patient to hold their arms straight at 90° shoulder flexion, and to keep them there with their eyes closed:
  — Any subtle weakness will be elicited by a gradual fall.
  — A 'drift' into pronation can be a sign of spasticity due to an upper motor neurone lesion.

- Sensation:
  - Use pinprick to test the anterolateral columns, testing each dermatome in turn, asking each time if the patient can feel a sharp sensation or merely pressure.

- Further tests:
  - Test the posterior columns with either vibrioception (tuning fork) or proprioception.
  - Proprioception can be difficult to test as patients sometimes find it difficult to differentiate between the movements of small joints even in the absence of neurology.
  - While vibrioception is rarely practised it is much easier to perform and interpret.
  - A few quick tips:
    — Never strike the tuning fork on your shoe or a table; either spring the ends together with your fingers and let go, or strike it against your thigh.
    — Start distally and work proximally, for example using the PIPJ of the index finger, then the second MCPJ, the radial styloid process, olecranon process, and finally the acromion.
    — Ask the patient if they can feel the vibrations.
    — If done swiftly you shouldn't need to restrike the tuning fork more than once during the testing of each limb.
    — Some neurologists prefer to test a patient's ability to identify when the vibrations cease but this then increases the overall time taken to perform this section of the examination.

Lower limb examination: inspection as described previously for the upper limb:

- Tone:
  - Test both at the hip and the knee.
  - To test hip flexion, gently perform internal and external rotation while the patient's legs are in the resting position. It is important to do this slowly to prevent involuntary reflex muscular contraction which may mimic increased tone.

- Tone at the knee should be assessed by almost interlocking your fingers under the lower part of the thigh and smoothly lifting upward to flex the knee. This should be performed at different speeds alternating rapidly between fast and slow to ensure there is no element of voluntary muscle contraction and assistance from the patient.

- Clonus:

  - This is an integral aspect of the lower limb examination but not expected in the upper limb examination.

  - Usually tested in the ankle, but can also be assessed in the thigh.

  - To assess ankle clonus, rapidly dorsiflex the ankle and hold the foot in a position of maximal dorsiflexion, ie approximately 90°.

  - To assess quadriceps clonus, hold on the anterior aspect of the thigh and pull down inferiorly towards the patella, again holding your hand in at the most inferior aspect of the motion.

  - Up to five beats of clonus is within normal and you should practise on healthy patients. Sustained clonus is considered to be abnormal and would be a sign of an upper motor neurone lesion.

- Power:

  - Assess using the same MRC grading, working from L1 to S2.

- Reflexes:

  - Assess the knee and ankle jerks.

  - To assess the knee jerk, place your left forearm under their partially flexed knee and strike the patella tendon directly.

> Some patients do not have an obvious patella on inspection due to overlying and adjacent soft tissue so palpate the area before eliciting the reflex.

  - To assess the ankle jerk, there are several acceptable methods but all involve holding the foot maximally dorsiflexed, with a partially flexed knee:

    — Strike the sole of the foot directly with the tendon hammer.

    — Perform the above with your hand held over the heads of the metatarsals and strike your hand.

    — Strike the Achilles tendon directly.

- Coordination:
  - Clear instructions are vital here: 'I would like to test some of the movements of your legs'; 'Please run the heel of your right foot up and down your left shin.'

Always assess gait, typically at the end of the examination.

PITFALLS

- Fasciculations are difficult to see at the best of times, so ensure you give yourself the best chance of seeing them by having a well-lit environment and looking at the larger muscle groups, for example the biceps/brachioradialis in the upper limb and the quadriceps group in the lower limb.

- Tone is often difficult to assess, with many patients finding it an effort to relax in the setting of the exam. Increase your chances of a good examination by adopting a friendly, confident but sensitive approach to quickly build a good rapport with the patient so they feel comfortable and relaxed.

Rest station:

- An important station, definitely not one to waste.

- Forget about any previous difficult stations, no matter how disastrous – you can't change the mistakes you have already made, but if you pull yourself together there's always a chance you could boost yourself back above the overall pass mark.

- Think about the stations left, especially the next one – what are the commonest cases for the station? Which parts of the examination do you normally forget? Think your way through the examination.

- Check your shirt, suit or dress to make sure you still look presentable.

Presentation (see Chapter 9, 'Active answering') is certainly an art, and an excellent opportunity to make up marks lost during a poor examination. Thank the patient, cover the patient up and then turn to face the examiners, as there is nothing more annoying than a student who keeps glancing at the patient rather than maintaining eye contact. Stand with hands behind your back and hold your stethoscope, ie do not hang it around your neck. Try to answer the question posed – are you being asked to present your findings or to give your differentials?

Never ever argue with the examiners – they are *always* right. *Smile* – not too much, but now and again, just to show that you're really a good person but this is a bad day to meet you for the first time!

Summary

● Examinations require lots of practice to appear smooth and assured.

● An orthodox examination is vital; even if your instructions to the patient are unclear, they will often know what it is you would like them to do as they have been subjected to countless examinations.

● Practise your verbal instructions for each examination routine, particularly the cranial nerve examination.

● Learn the list of bedside investigations that you would like to request after each type of examination.

● Practise, practise, practise – the skills discussed in this chapter can only be improved through examining lots and lots of patients.

● Don't forget to practise presenting your findings to a fellow student or doctor.

CHAPTER 6

OSCE stations: smaller systems, unusual stations

How to use this chapter

The major systems OSCE examinations are treated by students with a healthy degree of respect and fear, and rightly so, as they form the mainstay of day-to-day practice for graduated doctors. They also require a great deal of experience to identify signs and form a cohesive diagnosis, but ironically students tend to be well versed in these examinations because of their importance. In contrast, the examination of smaller systems, such as joints, eyes and skin are comparatively less familiar to students as they are not routinely examined on the wards, and tend to only be taught and tested in specialty attachments. Therefore we have created a comprehensive guide to these smaller systems, particularly for students who have not gathered much experience in them, and do not have a well-oiled system for performing them as yet.

Another feature of many medical school finals are unusual OSCE stations such as blood transfusion or prescription errors. These stations are designed with a view to patient safety; examiners want to ensure that doctors can manage the practical side of medicine as well as having the required knowledge base. We provide both the factual information required, as well as practical advice for managing these hands-on stations.

Joint examinations

Joint examinations are one of the often neglected areas of practice for OSCE examinations, and we will cover both the principles and the details in this section.

General joint examination advice

The basic principle of joint examination follows a 'look, feel, move' pattern followed by some special tests.

Before you begin, consider what can go wrong with joints, and therefore what options you are looking for. Common conditions for finals include osteoarthritis, rheumatoid arthritis, psoriasis, gout or specific joint problems such as medial meniscal tears in the knee. You are unlikely to see acute conditions such as fractures or septic arthritis. We have therefore included a list of possibilities before each test. Bear these in mind before undertaking your examination and it will guide you as to what signs to look for.

Ask the patient if there is any area which is painful, or any movements which cause pain. By the time you reach the finals, you may be used to practising joint examinations on 'well' patients or colleagues, but students often have surprisingly little experience of patients with active joint problems. Therefore, you may find it helpful to err on the side of caution when it comes to how vigorously to manipulate a limb in medical finals.

> Always examine the normal side first, and then compare this to the pathological side. This allows you to compensate for any normal variants in patient anatomy.

In the **looking phase**, ensure that the patient is properly exposed and you look at the joint from all angles. In the lower limbs, this may mean asking the patient to turn around and examining them from behind. Also with regards to the lower limbs, observation of the gait is important to pick up any functional issues which may hint at pathology.

The **feeling phase** is another opportunity to demonstrate your systematic nature. Start by feeling around joint lines for pain, following defined pathways which we have listed under each joint.

The **move phase** is further divided into active and passive movements, depending on whether or not the patient is able to complete the full range of movement, or is stopped by pain. Avoid using jargon, in particular the technical names for movements such as flexion or extension; rather, practise saying 'bend' or 'straighten'.

Verbal instructions must be especially clear in the joint examination stations compared to other OSCE stations. This is because they involve active participation on the part of the patient to a larger degree compared with the more passive major OSCE systems. Therefore we have included sample phrases under each examination which you can use or adapt, which may be useful in instructing your patients during the examination. Use these as a starting point, but bear in mind that the more you practise, the more you will see which instructions are easy to follow and which more obscure, and you will be able to refine your communication accordingly.

 Demonstrating the movements to the patients can be helping in aiding your instruction.

Each joint will also have 'special tests' for individual muscles or ligaments. Ensure that you learn them carefully, and we recommend that, if possible, you should remember the names of the tests as well, as your examiners will commonly be surgeons who may like to hear the formal nomenclature.

Anatomy as a subject is not specifically tested in medical school finals, and usually examinations will be undertaken in earlier years, if at all. However, relevant clinical anatomy remains a legitimate area for testing, and may be featured in the form of short questions in OSCEs. Therefore we have included some core anatomical facts which are commonly tested in examinations, to save you from having to trawl through anatomy books in the run-up to finals.

Shoulder

Possible pathologies: 'frozen shoulder', tendency for dislocation (unlikely to have a truly dislocated shoulder), painful arc syndrome.

Look for: muscle mass, any obvious asymmetry, scars (previous surgery) or skin changes.

Feel for: palpate the clavicles starting from the midline sternoclavicular joint, along to the acromoclavicular join laterally, for any joint line tenderness or fractures.

Move: flexion at the shoulder ('Raise your arms up in front of you'); extension at the shoulder ('Lift your arms up behind you'); abduction at the shoulder ('Lift your arms up to the side, and over your head'); internal rotation ('Bend your elbows to 90 degrees, and move your hands towards your stomach'); external rotation ('Keep your elbows bent and tucked in, and push your hands out to the side').

Special tests

Supraspinatus test – otherwise known as the 'emptying can' test ('Please could you hold your arms out in front of you as if you are holding two cans. Now please empty the cans. I will push down on your arms, please push up against me and tell me if it is painful').

This tests for impingement of supraspinatus which initiates the movement of abduction at the shoulder.

Gerber's 'Lift-off' test. Stand behind the patient. ('Please could you place your hands behind you and push me away').

This tests for rupture or dysfunction of subscapularis which carries out internal rotation at the shoulder. If the patient is able to push you away, then the test is positive.

Shoulder apprehension test. Elbow should be flexed to 90° and shoulder abducted to 90°, and you should hold the patient's humerus with one hand, while attempting to externally rotate the shoulder. Apprehension or pain is a positive sign.

This test is used to detect shoulder instability, and should come with careful instructions to the patient. ('As I move your shoulder, please tell me if you are feeling any pain and I will stop').

Winging of scapula ('Please could you place both hands on the wall and push'). This tests for the long thoracic nerve, which supplies serratus anterior, a muscle which holds the scapulae against the thoracic wall. It can be damaged in surgery, eg breast cancer surgery.

Associated knowledge

The muscles of the rotator cuff are teres minor, infraspinatus, supraspinatus and subscapularis. They support the joint and give rise to an area of weakness inferiorly, and thus it is commonly dislocated in this direction.

Hip

Look for: muscle bulk of quadriceps for wasting, and gluteal muscles.

Gait analysis ('I would like you to walk towards the back of the room, and then turn around and walk to me'). Look for a shuffling gait, or an antalgic gait whereby the patient avoids weight bearing on one of their limbs (a limp).

Trendelenburg sign. You are testing for weakness of hip abductors: gluteus medius and minimus. Ask the patient to stand on one leg, and observe their pelvis. In normal patients, it should rise on the opposite side of the standing leg, but a positive Trendelenburg sign is when the pelvis drops on the opposite side.

True length of legs. Remember that this is the anterior superior iliac spine down to the medial malleolus, whereas apparent leg length is from the umbilicus to the medial malleolus.

Feel for: you will be unable to palpate the joint itself as it is a deep structure. However, you can palpate the adjacent structures for pain or deformity, including the anterior and posterior iliac spines, and trochanters of the femurs.

Move: flexion ('Please bring your knee towards your chest as far as you can').

Internal and external rotation ('Please keep your knee in this position, and I will rotate your leg').

Abduction ('Please move you leg out to the side away from your body').

Adduction ('Please move your leg back towards your body, and across to the other side').

Special tests

Thomas test. This looks for fixed flexion deformities at the hip and is undertaken by effectively reducing the lumbar lordosis in spine. Ask the patient to lie flat on their back, place your hand in the depression made by the lumbar lordosis, then flex one hip fully to eliminate the lordosis (which you will feel with your hand which remains under their back). If there is a fixed flexed deformity, then the other leg will become flexed at the hip.

Associated knowledge

Avascular necrosis. The blood supply to the hip runs through the capsule, and therefore intracapsular fractures can result in avascular necrosis of the head.

The three ligaments which stabilize the joint are the iliofemoral, ischiofemoral and pubofemoral ligaments.

Knee

Possible pathologies: osteoarthritis, previous surgery, eg cruciate ligament repairs, meniscal tears, ligament ruptures or instability.

Look for: look at the knee from the front, sides and back for scars, swelling, asymmetry or erythema.

Feel for: along the joint line for tenderness, feel for patellar tracking and crepitus in extension and flexion of the knee. Feel in the popliteal fossa for a Baker's cyst.

Check for an effusion. Milk any fluid down into the joint from the thigh, and perform either the patellar tap test (push down on the patella), or the bulge test (attempt to transmit pressure through the fluid from the medial to lateral compartments of the joint and vice versa).

Move: extension ('Please straighten your leg at the knee'); flexion ('Please bend your leg at the knee').

Special tests

Anterior drawer test. This tests the integrity of the cruciate ligaments which prevent anterior–posterior movement at the knee joint. Ask the patient to lie down and bend their knees to 90°. Then apply pressure on their foot to stabilize it ('I'm going to sit down on your foot'), and pull firmly towards you with both hands. If you feel a laxity, this is a positive anterior drawer and indicates a disruption of the anterior cruciate ligament.

Note that some consultants advise against sitting on the patient's foot, as you are less able to control the pressure exerted and therefore are at risk of causing pain. Furthermore, patients with knee pathology often have pathology in other joints. If you prefer, you can firmly secure the patient's leg with one hand, while testing for anterior movement with the other hand.

Posterior drawer test. In the same position, inspect the patient's lower limb from the side. In cases of posterior cruciate rupture, the lower leg will visibly sag relative to its normal position. This should also be different from the contralateral side unless it is a rare case of bilateral pathology.

Tests which are unusual require you to explain, signal with your hands, and if necessary demonstrate to the patients very thoroughly. Ensure that you practise these diligently if you are to figure out the best set of words and gestures which can get your message across within the short OSCE time frame.

Medial and lateral collateral ligament stress test. Hold the leg of the patient in partial extension at the knee, and apply pressure in a valgus and varus direction. The patient will have pain or apprehension on the relevant side.

Associated knowledge

In addition to the cruciate ligaments, the knee also has strong collateral ligaments which prevent movement in the coronal plane.

Elbow

Possible pathologies: tennis elbow – lateral epicondyle, common extensor origin; golfer's elbow – medial epicondyle, common flexor origin; olecranon bursitis.

Look for: muscle mass; joint swelling or redness; nodules on the extensor aspect of forearm.

Feel for: tenderness; effusion; warmth. Palpate along the epicondyles and the olecranon.

Move: flexion ('Please bend your arms up at the elbow'); extension ('Please straighten your arms out'); pronation ('Please sit with your arms bent and palms facing upwards. Now, keeping your elbows tucked in, turn your palms over'); supination ('Please now turn your palms back to facing upwards').

Medio-lateral stability test. Lateral stability is tested by moving the forearm medially, while the humerus is internally rotated and the forearm is pronated, to minimize other compensatory movements.

Medial stability is tested by moving the forearm laterally, with the humerus in external rotation and the forearm in pronation.

In both cases, stabilize the upper arm with your other hand. If there is laxity present, this can represent instability of the respective collateral ligament.

Associated knowledge

The so-called 'carrying angle' is a natural valgus created when the elbow is extended, the forearms tend to angle out laterally. This is physiological.

The 'funny bone' is located on the medial epicondyle, where the ulnar nerve runs superficially. Minor trauma can cause the unusual sensations associated with the funny bone, but more severe trauma can damage this nerve which supplies the median 1½ fingers for sensation, and motor function to the hypothenar eminence and the intrinsic muscles of the hand.

Gait, arms, legs and spine screen (GALS)

The integral role of the spine in the locomotor system means that it is often assessed within the context of a full limb and gait screen, known as the GALS screen. This is used in practice, particularly from the surgical perspective, as well as settings such as rheumatology clinics, and may be featured as an OSCE station.

Possible pathologies: kyphosis/scoliosis, ankylosing spondylitis ('bamboo spine'), osteoathrititis, rheumatoid arthritis, disc pathology.

Gait

Look at stride length, antalgic gait (less weight on one foot), symmetry, turning circle (increased number of steps in eg Parkinson's).

Spine

Look from behind for muscle bulk paraspinally, scoliosis and iliac crest symmetry. Look from the side for kyphosis, check the lumbar lordosis and flexion ('Please could you try to touch your toes while standing'). Look from the front.

Feel for: tenderness of the spinous processes.

Arms

Look for: deformities of the fingers and hands.

Feel for: tenderness across the metacarpal heads by squeezing.

Movements: closing fist ('Squeeze my fingers') opposing thumb ('Touch your thumb to your index finger'); extension at elbows ('Put your arms out straight'); shoulder movements ('Put your hands behind your head').

Legs

Look for: knee swelling, muscle bulk.

Feel for: metatarsal head tenderness, knee crepitus.

Movements: knee flexion and extension ('Straighten out your leg'), hip rotation (passive; 'Put your knees up towards your chest, and I will rotate them around').

Special tests

Press on the midpoint of supraspinatus (found in the supraclavicular fossa of the scapula) for tenderness which might may suggest fibromyalgia.

Associated knowledge

Functional ability is the main point of the GALS assessment; impairment of finger opposition and grip weakness may make it difficult to perform movements such as doing up buttons or holding keys. Remember that rheumatoid arthritis is a likely cause of hand pathology, along with osteoarthritis. Shoulder problems are more likely to be muscular.

Hands

Possible pathologies: rheumatoid arthritis, osteoarthritis, Dupuytren's contracture, extensor tendon rupture (mallet finger). carpal tunnel syndrome, other neurological deficits (motor or sensory).

Look for: skin for rashes, nodules or atrophy; nails for pitting, ridging, pallor; muscles for wasting (check thenar and hypothenar eminences); bones for deformities; scars including carpal tunnel release; rheumatoid nodules along extensor aspects of forearms.

Feel for: warmth. Bimanually palpate each MCP for swelling or tenderness.

Piano key sign – push down on the ulna head; if this has significant depression, it is positive.

Test sensation of the ulnar, median and radial nerve by asking the patient to close their eyes and touching the little finger, index finger and first dorsal webspace respectively.

Move: wrists – flexion and extension ('Please press the palms of your hands together. Now touch the backs of your hands together'); fingers – flexion and extension ('Make a fist. Now straighten your little finger out. Now straighten all of your fingers'). Also test resisted abduction and adduction by asking the patient to keep a piece of paper in between two fingers. Thumb: abduction ('Please move your thumb towards the ceiling with your palm up').

KEY POINT

The hand examination may require you to demonstrate some of the required movements to the patient.

Hernia

It is fairly common to be asked to examine a hernia. There are many different types, of which the most common are epigastric, umbilical, incisional, inguinal and femoral. The most common of these are the inguinal herniae and we will describe an orthodox method of examining them which should allow you to comment on whether you think it is likely to be a direct or indirect type. It is vital to be familiar with the anatomy of the inguinal canal as it will assist you in your examination and is often asked about by the examiners.

Look for: ask the patient to stand up, inspect both inguinal regions carefully.

Location. Inguinal hernias form a swelling **above** the groin crease in comparison to femoral hernias, which protrude **into** the groin crease.

Extension. Look for extension into the scrotum.

Feel for: you should stand at the side of the patient and position yourself so that your examining arm is at approximately the same height as the inguinal ligament. Can you get above it? If you can, then it is likely to be a scrotal swelling rather than a hernia.

Define the swelling. Feel for the temperature, tenderness, approximate shape and size and consistency.

Is there an expansile cough impulse? Compress the swelling and ask the patient to cough. Feel for actual **expansion** of the swelling and not just an impulse.

Is the swelling reducible? Firmly press over the lump and then gently squeeze the lowest part. If it becomes less tense, gradually lift the entire swelling towards the external ring. If you succeed in reducing the hernia, slide your examining fingers along the canal to the internal ring to see if you are able to control the hernia by pressure here.

How does the hernia reappear? The direction of reappearance should confirm your suspicions regarding whether it is a direct or indirect hernia.

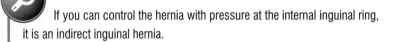

If you can control the hernia with pressure at the internal inguinal ring, it is an indirect inguinal hernia.

Further tests

Auscultate the swelling to hear for bowel sounds. Say that you would like to examine the other side and perform an abdominal examination to look for causes of raised intra-abdominal pressure such as ascites.

Uncommon OSCE stations

These stations are called 'unusual' as they do not fit into a major body system, and therefore there is not a overarching system that spans each one. In this section, look out for key points which you must undertake in order to score well in these scenarios.

Blood transfusion reaction

This OSCE station has been the feature of several medical school finals; given its severity, it is one that should be taken seriously.

This station is very much like a driving test in that you must know the rules of the station, and be seen to do them. This particularly applies to checking the numbers on the blood being transfused and also the patient's hospital number. It is no good looking at the pieces of paper and wristband intently; the examiner has no way to confirm that you are accurately matching up the numbers to each other. In order for you score the points for this station, you need to verbalize your actions:

'I will first stop the transfusion and perform an ABC assessment of the patient.'

'I would provide any required interventions which may include intravenous cannulation and fluid recuscitation, and I would also inform my senior, and consider the patient for ITU if appropriate.'

'Once they are clinically stable, I would then then check the numbers on the product unit. [Look at the screen.] One-eight-three-five-seventy. And on the wristband one-eight-three-five-seventy.'

It is absolutely vital to verbalize the numbers which are present, rather than just saying 'I will read them.' This is both for scoring in the OSCE, and also good clinical practice for when you are tired on a long shift, and have to deal with such important situations, as it can mean the difference between spotting or missing a discrepancy in the blood which was supposed to be given.

Additional tip: inform the laboratory. Remember, if this patient received an erroneous blood transfusion, calling the lab can prevent another patient receiving the bag destined for your patient.

Types of transfusion reaction

ABO transfusion reaction. This is a severe reaction caused by incompatible blood type.

Delayed transfusion reaction. This is an antibody-mediated response.

TRALI: transfusion-related acute lung injury, leading to pulmonary oedema.

Mild allergic reaction. A feature of this is urticaria; it can be treated with IV chlorphenamine and monitoring.

Massive transfusion. You may see 'iron overload' or 'hypothermia'.

The actual knowledge base for this station is not high, but if we consider why the station was introduced in the first place, it is to identify students who can deal with a relatively common and potentially very serious situation. Take all of the above steps to ensure you are seen to be safe, thorough and knowledgeable, and you will pass this station.

Urinalysis

Urinalysis stations can often combine practical and knowledge-based elements, or can test either one of these elements. Performing a urinalysis seems straightforward but there are some common pitfalls to avoid. Ensure that you have gloves and possibly an apron on while undertaking the urinalysis.

Dispose of the urine into the sluice and the urine containers into the clinical waste bins.

Timing is important in urinalysis. Ensure that you have a watch or clock visible, and rotate the urine dipstick container to compare the stick results with the colour key. Jot down the results as you go along.

> Ensure that you hold the urine dipstick in your non-dominant hand so that you can turn the container to check each result in turn, and also write down the results.

Additional knowledge

Be aware of specially requested tests which are available, eg pneumococcal antigen testing in pneumonia, or 24-hour collection of protein for VMA (catecholeamine breakdown product) for phaechromocytoma, which is a rare catecholamine-secreting tumour of the adrenal gland.

Cortisol levels in Addison's or Cushing's; a test would include a paired serum and urine cortisol level. The other blood test of note is U+E for sodium. Pregnancy tests are vital to undertake in cases of abdominal pain in women of childbearing age, and you may be asked about this. If the urine tests are equivocal, serum Hcg testing is indicated.

Renal stones will almost always have the presence of blood in the urine.

Nitrites are often thought to be the key indicator for UTI; however, a raised white blood cell count can increase your suspicions of a UTI if the patient is also symptomatic.

Peak flow/bedside spirometry

The main function of this test is to demonstrate that you can instruct and supervise a patient performing a peak flow test – which is a simple but significant test in respiratory pathology. Modern asthma treatment is guided by peak flow (as well as other factors) and the ratio of actual peak flow versus predicted peak flow (based on age) is the key figure.

Important points

When giving instructions, students often find it is helpful to talk about the theory of how to perform it, and then demonstrate it, giving the patient two opportunities to learn about the process.

Remember to be clear about what you are trying to ask the patient to do. With spirometry, remember to instruct the patient to 'Blow out all the air in your lungs', compared with peak flow, where you may say 'A short sharp burst, as hard as you can.'

Peak flow should be performed while standing. Give the patient a minute in between each puff to recover. Remember to take the best effort of three attempts.

 COMMON PITFALL

Actors are often trained to place their fingers over the marker of the peak flow device, so it will stop it at a low level. This is to ensure that you correct any 'poor technique' by asking the patient to repeat the test. Look out for this common trick!

Infection control/handwashing stations

C.Diff and MRSA are now the scourge of the NHS, and as such you may be called upon to demonstrate that you are able to fend off these pathogens as needed. This can be tested in medical finals as either infection control or a specific handwashing station.

You can draw upon hospital policies that you have seen on the wards.

Knowledge base

Unexplained diarrhoea (as opposed to confirmed infective diarrhea), is when the patient has a stool of Bristol stool type 6 or 7. Isolation in side-rooms remains a key intervention.

MRSA swabs are now standard for patients upon being admitted to hospital.

Other causes of unexplained diarrhoea

You may be given a scenario of what to do for a patient with unexplained diarrhoea. In such situations, make sure you describe all of the following steps.

- Isolate in side room.

- Send stool for culture.

- Check hydration status, and comorbidities, and give fluid replacement as required.

- Check drug charts for laxatives and antibiotics – these are two common causes of diarrhoea.

- Check drug chart for other changes or medications which could explain the diarrhoea.

- Stool chart – monitoring type and frequency of stool.

- Possible causes are C.Diff, Norovirus, infectious gastroenteritis. Enquire if any family members have become ill with abdominal pain, diarrhoea or vomiting.

Handwashing

It seems almost condescending to have advice on handwashing OSCEs, but year on year, people fail this station because they underestimate its importance to the examiners. This topic is vitally important; they are looking to see that you will be a safe doctor who practises good routine hand hygiene.

First, ensure that your handwashing technique is correct. Remember there are six main areas to cover:

fingertips;

fingers;

palms;

inter-digital spaces;

wrists;

thumbs.

Take your time, and be seen to cover all of these areas.

Remember to dry your hands thoroughly; there is often a mark on the OSCE mark sheet for this!

You may then be asked questions about hand washing, including:

'When can you use alcohol gel rather than washing?' [You can use it in between seeing patients' beds if you do not examine the patient, and if your hands are not soiled. You should wash your hands in case of physical examination, or if you have any bodily fluid exposure on the hands. You should also wash your hands when entering and leaving the wards.]

'What is the difference between hand washing and scrubbing?' [Hand washing is to remove the surface pathogens on the hands, whereas scrubbing is to remove the normal flora of endogenous bacteria which reside on our skin, to prevent their transmission during surgery.]

'Who is involved in the regulation of handwashing in hospitals?' [Everyone! The medical or surgical team should have a representative for infection control, and responsibility starts at the top with the consultant. There are also often infection control teams, and modern matrons who are involved in enforcing procedures, and all ward staff share this responsibility.]

Prescribing

Some medical school OSCEs now include a station where students are asked either to prescribe a number of medications onto a drug chart, or check a drug chart for common errors. This is clearly a very important attribute to test in terms of producing competent doctors, and is an OSCE station you should take very seriously.

Think about where and how examiners can trip you up. Errors in **patient identity**, **doses** or **methods of delivery** are the main serious events that can occur on the wards, and are therefore important to check and doublecheck on your charts.

Other stations have included insulin prescribing. Always prescribe units by writing the word in full, never abbreviating it to 'U'. Insulin often has its own specific prescription chart – but must also be prescribed on the patient's own drug chart.

Similarly to blood transfusions, make sure you enunciate each number or name to ensure that the examiner can see your thoroughness.

COMMON PITFALLS INCLUDE:

- Going too fast. Take your time to look over every square inch of the drug chart to try and find the error in the exam. Do not give the examiner the impression that you take it lightly or are in a hurry, as they are more likely to score against you if you seem like you would be an unsafe practitioner.

- Settling on a single error. OSCE stations five to 10 minutes long will often have several errors on a single drug chart – make sure you deal with the error as it emerges, but keep looking for any other possibilities.

Summary

- Joint examinations require practice and a base level of knowledge, including functional anatomy.

- Use friends, patients and colleagues to practise on to perfect your sequence.

- Always ask the patient about pain, and be alert for pain when moving their limbs.

- In the run-up to finals, focus on relevant anatomy rather than trying to revise the entirety of the syllabus again.

- Practise explaining and demonstrating the key movements to patients.

- Unusual OSCEs are specific stations testing particular skills, and are not routinely practised by many students.

- Ensure you are mentally prepared by reading through the key points and common pitfalls for each station.

CHAPTER 7

Simulations

How to use this chapter

In the same way that we advise you to recognize a different approach to revising for MCQs versus essay or short-answer papers, we strongly urge you to tailor your revision for OSCE examinations. As different as MCQs are from revising for medicine in general, revision for OSCE examinations should be similarly tailored. We devote a small chapter to developing well-rehearsed routines in OSCEs, for several reasons. First, medical school finals are stressful events, and if your usual calm is disturbed by panic or a sudden memory blank, going into a familiar and comfortable routine will allow you to perform on autopilot even under duress. More importantly, it will allow you to spend your energy and attention looking for signs and mentally constructing your presentation. This chapter details various practice activities you can undertake outside the ward, which are specifically designed to aid your OSCE performance.

What are simulations?

A simulation is a practice run-through of actions required to fully examine a patient for signs. All of these types of simulations can be undertaken with OSCEs from either the Major or Minor systems examinations in Chapters 5 and 6. We suggest making your simulations as realistic as possible. For example in the cardiovascular examination, time the pulse for the full 15 seconds each time, so that you get used to the feeling of time passing. In the OSCE itself, 15 seconds of silence feels like an eternity, and you need to condition yourself to this.

Always use a stethoscope where practical and listen to the (presumably) normal heart or lung sounds of your colleagues, rather than just placing it on their chest for show. This will again help you develop a feel for the timing of the examination sequence, as well as enhancing your muscle memory.

Always complete the full examination sequence. For example, testing for peripheral oedema in the cardiovascular examination should be undertaken. Don't simply say 'I would look at your ankles'; lift up the trouser legs and press down with your fingers.

> Make each and every simulation as realistic as possible and treat it seriously to gain the maximum benefit from this type of revision. Poor simulations can lead to poor habits in examinations!

Medic-to-medic simulation

This type of simulation is likely to be the most common, and involves one of your medical school colleagues acting as the patient, whom you will examine. You may have had medical school experience of this in clinical examination skills, and it is a good way to practise how to navigate the body looking for signs. This can be conveniently undertaken in medical school rooms as well as outside the medical environment.

Advantages:

- instant feedback from your peers;

- easy access to subjects;

- mutual learning experience.

Disadvantages:

- your patient may be too compliant and too familiar with processes;

- your patient may be too well known to you to provide a communications challenge, or provoke anxiety;

- working with colleagues with poor or incorrect technique can harm the development of your examination skills.

Simulating examinations which require exposure of the thorax may be easier to prac-tise on male colleagues while maintaining dignity. You may find it more appropriate not to expose the body during your practice.

> A big advantage of examining a medical student colleague is their ability to concoct pathologies and to play the part of a real patient. For example, they can simulate a patient with aortic stenosis, by verbalizing the results of your findings as you progress through the examination. As you listen to the heart, your patient will say 'You can hear an ejection systolic murmur.' This should prompt you to listen for relevant radiations, eg to the carotids. This way, both you and your colleague can revise patterns of signs in certain conditions.

Medic-to-friend simulation

While medical students are a convenient and abundant resource, they are not ideal patients as they will know the examination sequences themselves, and may tend to directly or indirectly assist you. Non-medical peers, such as students in other disciplines, or family members, can be useful practice subjects, as they will have almost no prior knowledge, and need formal instruction of how to move while you are examining.

This may help to tailor your language to a lay person, and such practice is a good screen if the words you are using are unclear to the average person, and gives you practice for dealing with situations. This is particularly important for the neurological and joint examinations, which can involve complex movements.

You can potentially do this type of simulation under observation from a medical colleague. This will allow you to practise presenting after examination, and give a more realistic OSCE feel with an examiner present.

Advantages:

- more realistic than medic-to-medic simulations;

- allows communication skills development and feedback.

Disadvantages:

- the patients cannot give you feedback on the OSCE examination itself;

- subjects may be less readily available than medical peers.

> Always ask your friend for feedback on your performance; it is important to understand how your patient felt, and they may be able to give useful pointers on how to put them more at ease, or identify areas where you can improve your communication.

Medic-to-inanimate simulation

> I used to practise examination skills on anything I could get my hands on, and when I was short of people, I used my stuffed toys!
>
> YK, Imperial College graduate

There may be times when you do not have a person readily to hand, but you wish to practise your OSCE. In this case, it can be helpful to have a dummy patient in the form of an inanimate object, which can be anything from a 2D drawing to a large pillow.

Some creative students have made a paper model of a patient to which you can stick labels of certain signs, eg in an abdominal case they have labels for spider naevi and jaundice. This will allow them to test themselves or a colleague on specific cases, and this can help to build up a repertoire of clinical reasoning – gathering signs together to formulate a diagnosis.

Advantages:

- allows you to practise OSCE situations at your convenience;

- retains some tactile and kinaesthetic element of revision.

Disadvantages:

- no real interpersonal interaction or normal signs;

- no feedback on communication skills.

Medic-to-psionic simulation

This type of simulation is a purely internal process by which you imagine the situation and systematically think about each element of the examination in sequence from start to finish. This can be out loud, or purely imaginative.

Advantages:

- this process reinforces the patterns of physical examination and allows you to develop a reflex process that can function even when you are tired and anxious;

- it can be undertaken anywhere – on the train or in a library. You can even stress-test your knowledge and recall by psionic revision in a crowded café;

- it is most helpful when coupled with your revision sheets for OSCE – so you can see the ideal sequence and notice what you missed.

Disadvantage:

- be wary of ingraining bad habits into your mind. Medic-to-psionic simulation should be the last process undertaken as there is no method of feedback other than internal analysis.

Summary

- Each element of medical school finals has its own particular characteristics and methods, and therefore revision should match this spectrum.

- Recruiting colleagues, friends, objects and your own mind to practise your OSCE routines are all methods to enhance your on-the-day performance.

- Be aware of the advantages and disadvantages of each simulation type.

- Those types with high levels of external input can be helpful initially to establish a well-constructed OSCE routine in terms of both sequence and language.

- Those types with less external input (eg medic-to-inanimate object, medic-to-psionic) can be used nearer to examinations to rehearse your techniques with less time and logistical requirements.

- Simulations complement your time on the wards spent looking for signs.

CHAPTER 8

Communication skills stations

How to use this chapter

Most medical schools have some examination stations which are particularly designed to test your communication skills; and in addition your interpersonal skills will be assessed in other OSCEs by looking at your interaction with the patients and your fluency of presentation.

This chapter aims to review the key elements of communication skills which you will need to demonstrate to examiners to gain the maximum available marks.

There is no shortcut to gaining proper communication skills for medical practice; you must spend time talking to and engaging with patients, as well as sitting in and seeing the variety of good and bad practice of qualified doctors, on the wards and in clinics. By the time you reach finals, you should have a good grasp of the basis of this interaction, developed from your scheduled medical school activities. However, in order to optimize your exam performance, we detail potential cases, techniques which you can use, and sample phraseology to allow you to see the theory of communication in action.

How to prepare

First, have a firm grasp of what is being tested. There are a number of specific stations which may be featured, and the common ones are listed below. The introduction of the OSCE format in exams was designed to increase consistency between examiners, but this does mean that they are looking for commonly important marking criteria. Therefore, each station described below has some key some skills which you can use that are helpful for the patients, but more importantly, are useful for you in the context of the OSCE.

Cynically, you might say that there is an element of acting involved in communication OSCEs, and to a degree that is true. You will be faced with actors role playing characters, which is a reasonable but not entirely accurate representation of a clinical encounter. In the same way, you can enhance your own performance with some elements of showmanship.

This starts with knowledge of the communication tools which are used in certain situations. For example, 'warning shots' and pauses in breaking bad news are useful tools, and you have to been seen to be using them in order to score the relevant marks. Therefore each station will have the *key processes* listed for you to use.

The second helpful type of information is sample phrases which we have found useful in our day-to-day practice, and indeed in medical school finals. Seeing actual sentences will help you to construct your own database of how to phrase what you are about to say to patients.

Lastly, some example cases and scenarios have been given to allow you to prepare in advance for the types of situation which may occur in your finals.

Explanation of a treatment or condition

These OSCE stations consist of many different types of diagnosis, which could be almost any disease. If the condition is chronic, severe or stigmatized, such as diabetes, epilepsy or cancer, you may wish to draw upon the principles of breaking bad news seen in the following case. For less psychologically impactful conditions such as kidney stones or simple cysts, the explanation element will be more important.

Start by assessing the patient's current state of knowledge. (Consultations for patients with a great degree of existing knowledge will be different from those with no prior knowledge.) Use open questions such as 'What do you know about cancer of the lungs?'

When explaining a treatment or a new condition, use a 'chunking and checking' technique. This means breaking up the information into smaller chunks, and after delivery of each one, checking with the patient that they understand before moving on.

Look around the station for pen and paper. If this is present, you may consider using this to write down medical terminology or use simple diagrams to explain concepts.

Ask the patient to explain the concepts back to you, to demonstrate their understanding and retention.

Give them the opportunity to ask questions actively. Prompt them if necessary, eg 'Do you have any questions for me at this stage?'

Avoid using medical jargon.

Preparation for this can involve lay explanations for concepts such as statistics. For example, when talking about risks, rather than express small specific percentages, you may consider saying 'Less than one in a hundred people who undergo this operation will experience this side effect.' Rather than stating a five-year survival score, you may wish to say 'After five years, the majority of patients will still be alive if they have the treatment.'

Be ready to clarify terms such as common, uncommon or rare.

At the end of the consultation, let the patient know that there is no imminent pressure to make a decision. You may wish to advise them to reflect, eg 'Have a think about what we discussed today, and talk to your friends and family. When we have our next appointment, we can discuss it further, answer any more questions, and if you have decided you can let me know then.'

> I was caught making up a percentage risk about prostate surgery because I didn't memorize all the surgical complications – and my examiner came down really hard on me for that.
>
> KL, Cambridge University graduate

There are two main ways to avoid KL's gruelling experience. The first is careful preparation of explanation stations by looking up what you will need to tell the patient, and working on how you will deliver this. This will allow you to tackle most of the concerns which patients may raise during your consultation. The second is practising how to navigate questions which occur and to which you do not know the answer, despite adequate preparation. Here are some useful tactics which you can employ.

> 'I'm afraid I don't know the chances of that happening myself. However, my consultant is next door and at the end of our consultation I can ask him for you.'

> 'I'm afraid I don't know the exact answer to that. I can find out for you so that we both know the exact figure if you like.'

Telephone consultation with senior doctor

Scenarios

OSCE stations can involve fake or even functioning phones, on the other end of which is a surly registrar or consultant. You may be given a case scenario, typically about a deteriorating patient on the wards, and usually many results will be available, including standard observations, as well as blood results. The case will often call for you to inform a senior of the situation and ask for a review of the patient.

This station is testing two skills – the first of which is your own analysis of the case, and how to structure your telephone appeal in the most useful and direct manner. The second is the communication side, which looks at how to cope with issues which arise from the conversation. This could be rudeness, lack of time or simple stubborn refusal from the senior, and it is up to you to convince them to come.

You can circumvent some of the problems by having a clear presentation of the facts, and having the information you may need.

Try the following pattern.

Introduction of the patient with a one-line summary, eg 'I have a 40-year-old patient who presented with a severe pneumonia three days ago.'

Next, quickly **explain the problem** and give supporting reasons: 'I would like your opinion as she is deteriorating rapidly, with sats dropping to 84%, with a depressed GCS of 13.'

Finally, give your **reason for urgency**: 'She has a tachycardia of 120 bpm and her blood pressure has fallen to 90/50 despite two litres of intravenous fluid. Since this has all happened over a short period she looks to be in septic shock and may be a candidate for ICU for ionotropic support. I would appreciate if you could see her as soon as possible, please.'

After your opening speech, the OSCE has just begun, and you will be required to answer a series of questions which may be asked in an aggressive or derogatory way. Remember to keep your cool, and have all of the results you may need to hand.

The senior may attempt to put you off until later, telling you to observe the patient for an hour and report back to them at that point. Under these circumstances, you need to have convinced yourself of why this patient needs an urgent or immediate review, so you can better express this to the senior. Therefore the preparation phase of this station is vital.

Inform your colleague of time frames and temporal relationships, as well as any co-morbidities which may add to the severity of the predicament, to aid your plight.

Convincing a senior to review a patient is something of an art, and you may have seen junior doctors attempting to do this on the wards, or have heard their complaints in a difficult situation. The key to such engagements is to stay focused on the patient, and organize the information which you are giving. Highlight critical signs, symptoms or results which are red flags for rapid deterioration.

Sexual history

Taking a sexual history is a challenging communication station and is usually poorly practised amongst medical students. Students from backgrounds or cultures where sex is not very well discussed may find it particularly challenging, and to save yourself and the patient from embarrassment, try to get as much practice as you can, as well as preparing questions in advance.

Potential cases include patients who have unusual genito-urinary symptoms, or patients who have health concerns secondary to a particular sexual encounter.

Approach delicate subjects with diplomacy. Enquiring about intimate details can be difficult and embarrassing to ask, but are critical for diagnosis. You can defuse potentially accusatory questions with phrases such as 'This a question I ask to everyone,' or 'I have a few routine questions for you.'

It can be helpful to maintain the professional barrier during the interview, with phrases such as 'This is information that may be important in the diagnosis and treatment of your condition', reassuring the patient why you are asking such personal questions. Alternatives such as 'This may be important for your health' can also be used.

You can also try to preventatively use phrases such as 'I have some further routine questions, but before I ask you I would just like to remind you that everything we discuss today will be completely confidential.' This can be a good lead-in to questions about extramarital activities in particular.

Once you have established rapport with the patient, it is important to enquire how they are feeling about the episode. For example 'What concerns do you have about this encounter?' This will help you engage with the non-medical aspect of the consultation.

Important facts to try and elicit include:

- number of sexual partners;
- nature of the sexual activities;
- use of barrier contraception;
- additional risk factors, including open wounds.

Respect the privacy of the patient if they are adamant in refusing to disclose certain details; this shows examiners that you are practical and would not risk the loss of all rapport in pursuit of a single detail.

Obtaining consent

Consent for surgery is a legal requirement, and stations in medical finals often feature an official-looking consent form. Due to the requirement of doctors knowing the risks of the operation, information on these stations is sometimes released one to two weeks before the exam to allow adequate preparation.

KEY POINT

Prepare both the factual information and how to explain it in lay terminology.

This station has a number of formal requirements due to the serious nature of the procedure being tested. Ensure that you undertake the following steps. Consent forms require you to write down the name of the operation. Ensure that you do this in full including the side of the operation, eg 'left-sided below-knee amputation'.

You must explain the serious and common risks; however, this does not mean every single risk.

The best resource for advice on consent forms is the people who fill them in on a daily basis; check with surgeons, gastroenterologists, or whoever would carry out the relevant procedure, that your list of risks is correct. You can also ask them to demonstrate how they would explain this to a patient, which can be an invaluable experience.

Use chunking and checking to confirm that the patient is following the process, and give time for them to ask any questions both during the event and at the end of the consultation.

Breaking bad news

This type of station is a very common exam topic, and comes in two different types depending on who you are breaking the bad news to. We will cover consultations with both the patient themself, and also with relatives.

The first type of scenario tends to be breaking bad news to a patient regarding a diagnosis. Common exam conditions include terminal diseases, eg metatstatic cancer, or long-term debilitating or stigmatizing conditions such as epilepsy, multiple sclerosis or HIV.

Important points which you should demonstrate during the course of this interview with both patients and relatives include:

- Establish the patient's concerns first. Open questions such as 'How are you feeling about your illness?' or 'Is there anything which you are particularly worried about?' may prompt the patient to discuss their own fears.

- 'Warning shots' are verbal cues that you are about to break the bad news, and allow the patient time to mentally prepare themself. Simple phrases such as 'I'm afraid I have some bad news' coupled with an adequate pause, can serve as a useful warning shot.

- Timing of pauses is an important step in managing the patient's initial shock. Give the patient time to absorb the information, and do not rush or pressure them with questioning.

- Demonstration of empathy involves both verbal and non-verbal elements. As part of allowing them space, you may wish to use compact statements such as 'I'm very sorry' or 'I'm so sorry.' Longer phrases can also be used such as 'I can't imagine what you are feeling right now', but balance these with the shorter phrases to keep pressure off the patient.

- Do not overact with physical gestures, and be cautious; any moves which could be misconstrued as inappropriate could give you an immediate fail.

- Adequate explanation of 'what happens next' can occur once the patient has dealt with the initial shock of the news. Try to keep this down to the key facts such as prognosis and treatment options available.

- Concluding the session can be helped by discussing the follow-up options and things such as palliation or support groups, which gives a forward-looking finish to the consultation.

Angry patients; managing complaints

The angry patient, who may or may not wish to make a complaint, is a scenario designed to test your skills of diplomacy and negotiation. Set-ups can include patients who have been waiting for a long time, or those who challenge your ability or decision making as a professional.

The primary goal of the initial interaction is to acknowledge the emotions that the patient is displaying. The patient may volunteer the cause straight away, or you may wish to explore the cause with the patient, eg 'I can see you're quite upset, sir, can I ask what is troubling you?'

In the first instance, you should make an apology to the patient. This does not necessarily constitute a personal apology for something that you have done to the patient, but it is an expression of empathy towards the patient, and you are sorry that a negative event has happened to them.

For example, in the case of a patient who has been waiting for a long time, you may wish to say 'I'm sorry for the long wait' or 'I'm sorry you've been kept waiting for so long.'

Next it is important to be clear what a patient is upset about. Common problems include waiting times, rudeness of staff and disagreeing with the courses of treatment offered.

Summarizing back to the patient can help to show your active listening and attention. This technique is commonly a feature of history taking, but in the case of an angry patient, you are trying to summarize the root of the problem. For example: 'Can I check with you that I understand? You are upset because a doctor has told you the likely cause of the disease, but now someone else has given you an alternative diagnosis.'

Managing complaints in OSCEs is a process in the same way as in clinical practice; **clarify** the concerns of the patient, **explain** the situation, **offer** diplomatic solutions and **advise** them of their rights and the complaints procedure if they still wish to go ahead.

Your role may be that of a mediator if the complaint is directed at a colleague. Under such circumstances, remember to maintain your professionalism, and to take your time to give a thorough answer if asked for a second opinion. Pay particular attention to giving clear clinical reasoning.

Remember that you are being tested as a junior within the system, and it is fine to not have all the answers on the tip of your tongue. You will be expected to be honest and forthcoming with this, and you should know when to consult a senior or refer on to a specialist.

You need to be aware of your own visceral reaction; being confronted with a hostile, rude or aggressive individual will trigger your sympathetic nervous system and you will feel agitated.

You can advise patients that there are patient advocacy organizations that help support lay persons in any complaints which they wish to make.

Hospitals will often have legal teams attached to them, but complaints in the first instance are usually dealt with by ward managers and department heads.

Inappropriate patients

Innappropriate patients are one category which has been rarely reported in finals. You may be propositioned with invitations of a social nature, and you should deal with these in a polite but professional way, eg 'Thank you for the offer, but I think we should concentrate on the matter at hand.' However, if the patient continues to press on, it may be best to take a firmer hand, eg 'Sir, I am here to assist with your health but I do not engage in social activities with my patients for professional reasons. Please can we continue with your medical issues?'

Summary

- Most students think they are good at communications skills – and while this is generally true, examiners are looking for demonstrations of particular techniques, not simply good conversationalists.

- Revise the relevant techniques, and practise applying them.

- Think of how you will phrase difficult questions, and try them out on colleagues.

- It is not enough to simply write down phrases – actually verbalize them to make it easier to remember them under exam conditions.

- Difficult stations such as sexual history require careful preparation.

- Taking consent stations can be improved by asking doctors to show you how they would obtain consent from patients.

CHAPTER 9

Active answering

It is rare to be taught how to answer questions concisely and insightfully, yet the examiners will frown and sigh as you meander your way down a steep path, digging all the while towards an early exit. You are expected to somehow pick up the art of answering questions through medical school, but here we will guide you through the theory of constructing a good answer, and then illustrate it with some worked examples.

Different question types

Answering an open-ended question may seem frightening but actually allows you to direct the discussion around areas that you are comfortable with and in which you possess a good knowledge base. It is important to try to give structure to your answer through the use of signposting to make the answer easier to understand and for important sections to stand out.

In an ideal situation you grasp immediately what the examiner is aiming at. For example, when asked 'Which investigations would you like to request?' after presenting a case of community-acquired pneumonia, you can the target your answer towards: a) confirming the diagnosis; b) assessing the severity; c) ruling out differentials; d) elucidating the cause/organism.

Unfortunately you won't always understand what the examiner wants, and if asked a question which you are not sure about, you should have a system or safe method of answering – otherwise your answer sounds very vague and not really directed anywhere in particular. There are several generic question types which we illustrate with worked examples.

Generic question types include open descriptive, list type, asking for a summary of relevant investigations and management, asking about complications of a procedure or condition, and asking for a summary of clinical findings in an OSCE setting.

Open descriptive

Examples:

- Tell me about endocarditis/headaches.

- What do you know about respiratory failure?

The above question type is briefly scary but actually provides you with the space to say only as much as you know, and to gloss over those areas which you aren't sure of. You have been given the freedom to construct an eloquent, interesting answer around only those areas of the topic that you feel confident about.

This type of question is primarily used as a test of thinking under pressure. The examiners would like you to demonstrate clarity of thought and a structured approach.

It is important to have a generic model with which to answer any open question. One example structure is shown below:

- Introduction

- Definition

- Incidence, sex distribution, ethnicity

- Types, classes

- Causes, risk factors

- Symptoms

- Signs

- Differentials

- Investigations

- Severity

- Treatment

- Complications

- Prognosis

> Even if you forget or are unable to talk about some of the subheadings, your answer as a whole will sound a lot more logical and considered.

A worked answer is shown below.

Q) Tell me about subarachnoid haemorrhage as a cause of headaches.

A) Subarachnoid haemorrhage is a life-threatening cause of headache and results from bleeding into the subarachnoid space. 80% are caused by rupture of saccular aneurysms and 15% are caused by the rupture of arterio-venous malformations.

Risk factors include smoking, hypertension and chronic alcohol abuse.

Classic symptoms for a subarachnoid haemorrhage are of a sudden onset occipital headache with vomiting and neck stiffness, with drowsiness and confusion seen in severe cases.

Signs on examination are often minimal, with some patients displaying photophobia and neck stiffness resulting from meningeal irritation, and others merely drowsy with no focal neurology.

Differentials of a severe headache include infections such as meningitis, tumours, cerebrovascular accidents and inflammatory conditions such as temporal arteritis. Differentials of drowsiness or confusion include poisoning, metabolic causes such as diabetic ketoacidosis and sepsis.

First-line investigations include CT head to look for a fresh haemorrhage in the subarachnoid space, and lumbar puncture following this if the CT is negative.

Severity is graded by signs, with grade 2 having neck stiffness and cranial nerve deficits and a mortality of 11% and grade 5 being comatose with a 100% mortality.

Treatment is primarily neurosurgical, with options including clipping and coiling the aneurysms. Medical therapy includes careful blood pressure control, analgesia and nimodipine to prevent vasospasm.

A structured, well-phrased answer scores many more points than a long, rambling answer. You are not going to be given the time to go through all of the above answer, and should therefore be prepared for interruptions. However, these questions should hopefully be based on the structure you have provided and therefore you should have something interesting to talk about.

It is most likely that the examiners will use an open descriptive question to break the ice after you have presented your findings, to allow you to demonstrate some knowledge of the subject in question before they ask more specific questions.

On closer inspection of the above example, note the use of signposting to create shorter paragraphs which are more easily understood by the examiner.

List type

This question type is most often used with respect to aetiology (causes) or types of a disease. It is important to make a rapid decision on the approach you are going to take for the particular topic being examined, for example in terms of frequency, severity, anatomically or physiologically.

It is vital that you have a standard list of causes that you apply to any condition to act as an aide memoire. Often known as a 'surgical sieve', this list essentially covers all major causes of any possible disease. An example sieve is shown below.

Congenital and acquired causes, with 'VITAMIN' acting as a mnemonic for the acquired causes.

- Congenital

- Acquired

  - Vascular

  - Infectious/Inflammatory

  - Trauma/Toxins

  - Autoimmune

  - Metabolic

  - Iatrogenic

  - Neoplastic

A front-loading approach is to give the two or three most important (in terms of either frequency or severity) causes and then to proceed in a structured manner based on anatomy, physiology or according to a surgical sieve.

A worked example is shown below.

Q) Tell me about the causes of chest pain.

This question must be answered in terms of severity rather than frequency given the potential life-threatening causes.

This type of question is more complex than those which do not require you to factor in severity as well as causes, such as the causes of hyperkalaemia, mitral regurgitation or bronchiectasis.

A) Life-threatening causes of chest pain include cardiac causes such as myocardial infarction, vascular causes such as aortic dissection and pulmonary embolus, respiratory causes include tension pneumothorax, and gastrointestinal causes include oesophageal rupture.

Other causes of chest pain include inflammatory such as costochondritis, pleurisy and myo or pericarditis. Infectious causes include pneumonia, empyaema and herpes zoster. Neoplastic causes include bony metastases, and gastroesophageal causes include reflux and oesophageal spasm.

Note that even though the answer is structured in terms of severity of condition, it is still broken down into different subcategories. By subcategorizing the causes your answer sounds much more structured and well thought out to a listening examiner, and is far preferable to simply saying the causes in order of which comes to mind first.

A good general approach is to start with two or three of the most important causes, usually due to severity, importance or frequency. Then go though the other causes by category, listing one or two causes in each.

Investigations

There is a method to the presentation of the relevant investigations. Examiners like to see a candidate present only the relevant investigations, and to list them in order of complexity, starting with simple bedside tests such as an arterial blood gas and ECG. The next level of tests are those which require a little more time to perform and to get the results, such as a chest radiograph or blood tests. Finally there are tests such as CT or MRI which are expensive, time consuming and need specialist interpretation.

Never simply list a number of blood tests without a clear reason why; if you are unlucky enough to be asked why you want to request liver function tests in a patient with pneumonia and you don't know, the examiners will not be impressed. While that in itself is a very minor mistake, they will now look with greater scrutiny at everything else you say in case you are just going through the motions without understanding why certain investigations are performed.

> Never request an investigation without knowing what an abnormal result signifies, and how it would alter your management.

Example:

Q) Which investigations would you request in this 48-year-old lady presenting with a community-acquired pneumonia?

- Venous blood for:
    - Full blood count – markers of sepsis;
    - Urea and electrolytes – signs of dehydration, hyponatraemia associated with legionella pneumonia;
    - Liver function tests – deranged in certain atypical pneumonias;
    - Blood cultures.
- Sputum for microscopy, culture and sensitivity;
- Arterial blood gas if the patient is breathless or has low oxygen saturations;
- Urine for pneumococcal and legionella antigens;
- Chest radiograph looking for consolidation and also complications such as a pleural effusion, empyaema and pneumothorax.

Putting this together into a cohesive and flowing answer is difficult, and one possible approach is shown below:

A) I would start with blood tests including blood cultures, full blood count, urea and electrolytes and liver function tests. I would request a chest radiograph and perform an arterial blood gas if the patient was breathless or had low oxygen saturations. I would request a sputum sample for microscopy, culture and sensitivity and a urine for pneumococcal and legionella antigen.

Management

When answering a question based on the management of a particular condition it is a great opportunity to show the examiner your detailed understanding of the nature of disease, its complications and the optimal treatment plan. Your answer will include some first-line investigations but you are not expected to produce an exhaustive list, merely demonstrate that you have an understanding of which are relevant in the initial management.

A worked example is shown below for the management of a primary spontaneous pneumothorax:

Q) How would you manage a patient who has no previous medical conditions presenting with their first spontaneous pneumothorax?

A) I would quickly assess the airway, ruling out any possible obstruction. I would give the patient 15L oxygen through a non-rebreathing mask. I would assess the chest to confirm the side of the pneumothorax and the absence of any signs of a tension pneumothorax. I would get pulse oximetry, blood pressure and three-lead ECG monitoring. In the absence of any clinical signs of a tension pneumothorax I would gain intravenous access, request a portable chest radiograph and consider whether the pneumothorax requires aspiration depending on whether the patient is breathless or there is more than 2 cm rim of air on the chest radiograph.

> While some knowledge of the BTS guidelines for the management of spontaneous pneumothorax is required, the bulk of the answer is drawn from 'first principles of management of the unwell patient', ie merely knowing the algorithm of the condition being tested is not sufficient to gain a pass.

Complications

There are several possible ways to structure this answer. Some examples are shown.

- Frequency:
    - common and rare.

- Severity:
  - life threatening and less severe.
- Location:
  - local and systemic.
- Temporally:
  - acute and chronic.

Using the example of pneumonia:

Q) Tell us about the complications of pneumonia.

A) Complications of pneumonia can be divided into local and systemic. Local complications include parapneumonic effusion, empyaema, abscess, pneumothorax, respiratory failure and ARDS. Systemic complications include atrial fibrillation, septicaemia, pericarditis and jaundice.

KEY POINT

There is a big difference between a pass and a distinction answer, and while that is sometimes knowledge based, in many instances it is simply the way you present and phrase your information that makes your answer appear more relevant, in depth and organized.

Worked examples

We use the topics of pneumonia and ulcerative colitis to illustrate further worked examples of the different question types. We have only shown the first line and early structure of each answer. If your first sentence is eloquent and front loaded then many examiners will be satisfied that you know the core of the material. They will have 'passed' you mentally and then be listening for any signs of a merit/distinction answer. Never repeat the question instead of answering it as this is extremely annoying for the examiner!

- Pneumonia
  - What are the different types of pneumonia? (List type)
  - The main types of pneumonia can be classed as community acquired, hospital acquired, in the immunocompromised patient and aspiration pneumonia.

- Tell us about pneumonia. (Open descriptive)
- Pneumonia is an acute lower respiratory tract infection with evidence of consolidation on a chest radiograph. Typical symptoms include breathlessness, fever, productive cough and pleuritic chest pain.

If the examiners don't stop you at this point then you have several choices depending on what your comfort zones are. For example, you could continue to talk about typical signs, and then which bedside investigations are helpful. You could talk about the different types of pneumonia or about the scoring system and management principles.

- What are other causes of breathlessness? (List type)
- Other respiratory causes of breathlessness include pneumothorax, pleural effusion, asthma and COPD. Cardiovascular causes include heart failure and pulmonary embolus. Metabolic causes include a metabolic acidosis due to diabetic ketoacidosis or salicylate poisoning.
- Why do we use the CURB65 score? (Management type)

The answer to any question about scoring is the same ... because it affects management!

- The CURB65 score stratifies patients into different classes of severity and helps guide antibiotic choice. Scores of greater than 2 are treated as an inpatient with intravenous antibiotics.
- Which antibiotics would you use? (Management type)
- I would use the CURB65 score to score the patient and then be guided by local trust policy. In this trust a community acquired pneumonia with a CURB65 score of 1 can be treated with amoxicillin 1g tds orally for 5 days as an outpatient.
- Tell us about respiratory failure. (Open descriptive)
- Respiratory failure is defined by a pAO2 of less than 8 on air, and can either be type 1 or type 2 depending on the presence of hypercapnia. Type 1 is primarily caused by a ventilation-perfusion mismatch, and common causes include pneumonia, pulmonary oedema and pulmonary embolus. Type 2 is primarily caused by alveolar hypoventilation and common causes include pulmonary disease such as asthma or COPD, reduced respiratory drive caused by sedation or head injury, and mechanical restriction caused by kyphoscoliosis.
- What is the management of pneumonia? (Management type)

- The principles are supportive oxygen therapy if the patient is breathless or has respiratory failure, antibiotics according to the CURB65 score and type of pneumonia, and admission to hospital based on criteria such as severity of pneumonia, respiratory failure and co-morbidities.
- What are the main complications of pneumonia (Complication type)
- Complications can be divided into local and systemic. Local complications include pleural effusions, lung abscesses and empyema. Systemic complications include sepsis which leads to hypotension and atrial fibrillation.

- Ulcerative colitis
  - Tell me about ulcerative colitis. (Open descriptive type)
  - Ulcerative colitis is a chronic condition affecting the colonic mucosa where episodes of inflammation affect the rectum or spread proximally to involve a variable length of colon. The prevalence is approximately 1 in 1000 and typically presents before the age of 30.
  - What are the typical features of a flare of ulcerative colitis? (List type)
  - A typical flare presents with bloody diarrhoea and crampy lower abdominal pain. Systemic features may be marked and include fever, weight loss and lethargy.
  - What are the extraintestinal manifestations of ulcerative colitis? (List type)
  - Joint involvement presents as sacroiliitis, ankylosing spondylitis and large joint arthritis. Skin changes include erythema nodosum and pyoderma gangrenosum. Ophthalmic signs are conjunctivitis, episcleritis and iritis. Hepatic involvement can cause primary sclerosing cholangitis and cholangiocarcinoma.
  - Which tests would you request in a patient presenting with an acute flare of ulcerative colitis? (Investigation type)
  - I would request blood tests including FBC, ESR, CRP to look at the degree of inflammation, U&E to assess dehydration and electrolyte imbalance and blood cultures if febrile. I would order an erect chest radiograph to rule out free air under the diaphragm and a supine abdominal radiograph to rule out toxic megacolon.
  - What are the Truelove and Witts criteria? (Open descriptive type)
  - This is a scoring system to assess the severity of a flare of ulcerative colitis, and uses features such as temperature, heart rate, haemoglobin and ESR. If assessed as severe, the patient may be best managed with intravenous hydration and steroids, rectal steroids and daily tests for inflammatory markers and toxic megacolon.

- Describe the management of an acute severe flare of ulcerative colitis. (Open descriptive type)

- Priorities are to carry out rapid rehydration with 1L normal saline, administer steroids in the form of 200mg hydrocortisone intravenously, take blood tests to aid the assessment of severity, and request an abdominal and erect chest radiograph to rule out toxic megacolon and bowel perforation.

- What are the complications of an acute flare? (Complication type)

- Complications may be life threatening and include toxic megacolon leading to perforation, and haemorrhage leading to hypovolaemic shock.

By examining the answers shown above you should be able to see patterns emerging regarding the construction of the answers.

Presenting clinical findings in an OSCE

A pass answer would be to identify the abnormality. A merit/distinction answer would go further and, without prompting, describe:

- The severity – often an accurate assessment is difficult without investigations, but it should be possible to class an abnormality into mild, moderate or severe.

- Presence or absence of complications – you should know the most common side effects of any condition, and therefore be on the lookout for these from the moment you begin the examination.

- A few possible causes – most candidates will know a long list of causes of any particular condition. You should aim to suggest the two or three most likely given the other physical findings on examination.

- A management plan – examiners are clinicians working in the real world and therefore understand and appreciate a considered plan for further investigations and/or treatment considerations.

Worked example A: patient with a previous renal transplant

Pass level:

Candidate: This patient has a J-shaped scar in the left iliac fossa and a palpable pelvic mass suggesting a renal transplant.

Examiner: What do you think is the most likely underlying diagnosis resulting in the need for a transplant?

Candidate: I think the presence of large bilateral renal masses suggests a diagnosis of polycystic kidney disease.

Examiner: Are there any signs of renal replacement therapy or the side effects of immunosuppressive therapy?

Candidate: There several arteriovenous fistulas on the left arm indicating previous haemodialysis. The patient looks Cushingoid and there are several areas of ecchymoses in keeping with chronic steroid therapy.

Examiner: Did you assess this patient's fluid status?

Candidate: The patient was euvoleumic.

Merit/distinction level. This patient has a scar and pelvic mass consistent with a renal transplant for presumed polycystic kidney disease given the bilateral enlarged kidneys. There are old fistulas on the left arm consistent with previous renal replacement therapy. The patient has a Cushingoid appearance and has multiple areas of bruising consistent with chronic steroid therapy. There was no sign of fluid overload.

Worked example B: patient with a pleural effusion

Pass level:

Candidate: This patient has reduced expansion at the left base with a dull percussion note and decreased air entry. I think they might have a left-sided pleural effusion.

Examiner: Which investigations would you like to perform?

Candidate: I would like to request a chest radiograph to confirm my clinical findings.

Examiner: Are there any other investigations you would like to request?

Candidate: I would like to aspirate the effusion and send the sample for analysis.

Examiner: Which tests would you request on the sample aspirate?

Candidate: I would like a protein level, microscopy, culture and sensitivity and cytology.

Examiner: Are there any other investigations you would like to perform?

Candidate: I would like to perform an arterial blood gas and venous blood tests.

Possible fail:

> Candidate: The patient has decreased air entry and a dull percussion note on the left side.

Analysis: Minimal examination findings presented to the examiner, and no attempt made to follow with further investigations or to offer any differentials.

> Examiner: What do you think this could be?
>
> Candidate: This could be a pleural effusion.
>
> Examiner: What would you like to do next?
>
> Candidate: I would like to aspirate the effusion and send the sample for analysis.

Use of ultrasound guided aspiration not mentioned. No effort made to discuss the tests to be performed on the sample aspirate.

> Examiner: Which tests would you like to be performed on the sample aspirate?
>
> Candidate: Erm... I'm sorry but I don't know.

Analysis: Never mention a test if you don't know why it is done or how it would change your management. One way to remember the tests is to think of the three laboratories involved, ie. Biochemistry (protein, glucose, pH, LDH), Histopathology (cytology) and Microbiology (microscopy, culture and sensitivity).

> Examiner: Which other tests could help you in this patient's management?
>
> Candidate: CT?

Analysis: A classic panic answer where the candidate has forgotten about the more simple bedside tests such as arterial blood gases and venous blood tests.

> Examiner shakes his head in silence and studies the mark sheet, hoping in vain to find any boxes which can be ticked as 'pass'.

Merit/distinction level:

> This cachectic patient has a left-sided pleural effusion as evidenced by reduced expansion, dull percussion note and reduced air entry at the left base. Given the nicotine staining of his fingers, pursed lip breathing, prolonged expiratory phase and cachexia I think a malignant pleural effusion is highly likely and would like to perform an ultrasound guided diagnostic aspiration. I would

send off the sample to biochemistry for protein, glucose, pH and LDH. I would also request cytology and microscopy, culture and sensitivity. The patient also requires venous bloods to include a serum protein level so we could determine if it is a transudate or an exudate.

Note that the merit/distinction answer can sometimes require slightly less detailed information as you have the initiative and can therefore choose to talk about what you feel comfortable being asked about. By comparison the pass answer requires more in-depth knowledge about more areas as the candidate must answer each question in turn and has no chance to blend two points together or gloss over a point they are unsure of.

The merit/distinction answer is a lot easier to hear as an examiner. It shows initiative and forward thinking by the candidate and the examiner has mentally passed you by the time you are halfway through the answer, and from there onwards is merely waiting to see if you can produce something to allow them to award you a merit/distinction.

> Practise 'thinking outside the box' when presenting clinical findings, and aim to comment on differentials, severity, causes and first line investigations.

Summary

- Always look to subcategorize your answer so that it appears more structured.

- There are always several different approaches to structuring any answer, so become familiar with rapidly deciding which approach to take.

- There is no right or wrong way to present your information; as long as you can justify it and your method is not too unorthodox the examiners will hear you out.

- It is always better to give less information in a structured fashion than simply blurt out a random list of causes or differentials.

- Practise the first line of the answer for the commonly asked questions in each topic as this sets the tone and structure for the whole answer.

- When presenting clinical findings in an OSCE, aim to summarize clinical findings in a concise manner including significant negatives. State your differentials, mention some possible causes, comment on severity and finally discuss several first-line investigations.

CHAPTER 10

How to learn and present imaging

How to use this chapter

X-rays, CT scans, MRI images and ultrasound scans are commonly viewed in every hospital, which makes them fair game for medical school finals examinations. Not only are they commonly featured in written examinations, but they can also be found in OSCE stations requiring verbal responses. This chapter details the process of learning how to identify key features of various modalities of imaging, as well as a methodical approach to present your answers either to your consultant on the ward or in an exam setting. After completing this chapter, you will never have to fear the dreaded early-morning radiology MDT again. We have divided the chapter into 'Learning imaging', which focuses on the range of activities that you can use, and 'Presenting imaging', which is concerned with the delivery of the information you have gleaned.

Learning imaging

'First do the norm'

Many students get used to seeing unusual pathologies and 'interesting' X-rays during teaching, but the first step to having a robust understanding of imaging is to actively learn about the normal. It is only by having seen dozens of normal radiographs and CTs that you will be able to quickly identify the abnormal findings. It also creates the correct attitude towards radiography – which is a tool used both to identify specific problems and to look for incidental findings. We therefore encourage you to spend plenty of time looking at chest and abdominal radiographs, arterial blood gases, ECGs and CT heads from the various sources which are listed under 'Learning resources' later in the chapter.

One of the most helpful activities you can undertake in 'normal-based learning' is to have multiple normal radiographs side by side to compare the spectrum of normality. In particular, pay attention to lung fields and abdominal gas patterns, as these areas exhibit the highest degree of normal variety. For each image, make sure you look at the surrounding anatomy, to ensure you are not missing any incidental findings.

KEY POINT

The 'normal' chest and abdomen show remarkable variety. Learning the normal will reduce the incidence of you falsely accusing a radiograph of harbouring pathology, and allow you to be more confident in your analysis.

Which investigations come up in finals?

The chest radiograph and the abdominal radiograph are two of the most frequently encountered and therefore you should spend a greater proportion of your time on these than other types of radiographs. Other common radiographs are focused on the bony periphery and include the pelvis, limbs and cervical spine.

CT head, and to a lesser degree thoracic and abdominal CT scans may also be examined, although they are less commonly featured, and MRI scans are mostly of the spine and brain. Although it is unfair to say that no other imaging may turn up in your examination, if you focus on the common types of imaging you should be able to tackle medical finals and indeed your foundation trainee years.

Chest radiograph

When reviewing a chest radiograph, you must carefully review all of the following areas:

- lung fields;
- cardiac outline;
- mediastinum;
- trachea;

- bones;

- soft tissues;

- presence of gas under the diaphragm.

We list below a number of systematic approaches to analyse the CXR.

'Outside-in approach'. This method starts peripherally, looking at soft tissue and bones, and works its way through the lung fields towards the mediastinum and trachea in the centre.

'Inside-out approach'. This method has the advantage of looking at areas which are more likely to have significant pathology in a CXR.

'Identification/review approach'. This approach is one which you might see used by practising doctors. First, identify any obvious pathology (typically in the lung field), and after describing it, move on to a systematic review.

Choose the systematic method for CXR review that you prefer, and then stick to it for looking, which will allow you to develop your pattern and perform this kind of review under the pressure of examinations.

For medical finals, particularly look out for:

- Shoulder pathology or mastectomy in CXR. This is a cunning examination technique, which can catch out students who only look at the lung fields but not the soft tissue and bone surrounding it.

- Ground glass appearances in pulmonary fibrosis.

- Apical pathology. TB can sometimes be represented in finals exams, and the apices of the lungs are often neglected by students.

- Abdominal pathology in a CXR. This is typically manifested as gas under the right hemi-diaphragm; you must always check this area as the consequences of missing a perforated bowel are very serious.

Abdominal X-ray

The AXR is arguably harder for medical students to learn, partly due to the fact that there is a far higher relative exposure to CXR, with most patients on medical wards and emergency departments requiring them as part of their care. In contrast, AXR is less commonly used, and will predominantly be seen on surgical wards. Therefore make the most of opportunities to review abdominal radiographs of patients with doctors on the ward, and try to identify pathology.

The other difficult aspect in comparison is that the CXR has a number of prominent features to divide up your review; you can look at each lung field in turn, and then on to the mediastinum, for example. However, the abdomen is a large area which is not naturally divided, which means you need to develop a formal system for analysis. The best way is to treat it like an abdominal examination, and to review each of the nine sections of the abdomen in turn.

Do not forget to review the spine, lower ribs, pelvic bones and para-lumbar region. For medical finals, look particularly for:

Gas pattern. Learn to identify the differences in large and small bowel dilatation patterns.

Look for position (central vs peripheral).

Presence of valvulae conniventes which span the complete distance of the small bowel.

Presence of haustra which extend only part of the way across the large bowel.

For small and large bowl obstruction, assess how large the dilatation appears to be, and remember that the threshold the maximum diameter of the large bowel is 55 mm, while the small bowel is 35 mm.

Renal pathology. You may be shown a KUB, which is an abdominal film showing the kidneys down the bladder. This type of film should raise your suspicions for the presence of a renal stone, which will be a bright white area, as such films are performed when the doctor has a clinical suspicion of a stone. The three most common sites for 'holdup' are at the pelviureteric junction, the pelvic brim and the ureterovesical junction.

You may be shown an intravenous urogram, where dye has been injected into a patient, and you will see a 'filling defect' if there is a block in the ureter, as the dye will not filter down past the blockage, as well as a 'standing column' of dye above the blockage. A normally functioning ureter will show almost no dye inside.

CT scans

CT head scans are quite frequently seen in medical school finals, and this reflects the need to rapidly identify significant pathology in practice. You may not expect to have CT scans of other areas, so CT head presentation should be the focus of revision for this particular imaging modality. You should still make the best use of your time on the wards, particularly surgical films, where consultants and registrars will review abdominal CT scans, but for medical finals, CT heads are the priority.

The common possible pathologies found on a CT head for medical students are listed below. In order to allow you to learn more about the key points of the conditions you may find, we have included some basic diagnostic and background information.

Extradural bleed. The dura mater is the outermost layer of the three meninges, is thick and tightly bound to the cranium. The bleeding vessel is arterial, but not derived from the circle of Willis. It is in fact from the middle meningeal artery, a branch of the external carotid. It runs under the temporal bone, and therefore blows to the side of the head can rupture the artery and cause extradural bleeds. Suspect this type of bleed with clinical history of trauma.

On CT scan, they appear as lens-shaped lesions on the periphery – this is because their tight binding to the cranium peels away under pressure from the blood near the artery, but at the edges the dura is still attached to the bone. The lens shape has a fat middle and thin edges due to this phenomenon.

Subdural bleed. These are venous bleeds which occur when the bridging veins of the skull are ruptured. These veins become stretched as our brain atrophies, either in old age or in conditions such as alcohol abuse, and falls or acceleration/deceleration injuries can cause tears of these veins and a subdural bleed. Suspect this type of bleed in the elderly or alcohol abusers.

On CT scan, they appear as semi-lunar (half-moon-shaped) lesions in the periphery, because unlike extradural haemorrhages, this bleed occurs into a potential space that is not tightly bound. This means that edges are not thin and the centre not too fat, and the blood is distributed more evenly, like a band.

Distinguishing between subdural and extradural bleeds requires a careful look at the edges of the lesions – and practice!

Subarachnoid bleeds. These occur from the circle of Willis, and the majority occur due to rupture of a berry aneurysm in this area. Some patients have a family history of aneurysms or connective tissue disorders such as Marfan's syndrome. Typically, they present as a sudden onset thunderclap headache, and can have signs of meningeal irritation (photophobia, neck stiffness).

On CT scan, the high attenuation area is central rather than peripheral, and can form an irregular shape, settling in the most gravity-dependent areas.

Additional tips and tricks for learning CT head

Look for midline shift of the brain, which appears as asymmetry. This can be most apparent in the ventricles. Midline shift indicates a mass lesion, and the danger is 'coning', particularly of the structures passing through the foramen magnum. The midbrain emerges from this point, and if the respiratory centres contained within it are compressed, this can cause coma and death.

Ring-like lesions could be either primary or metastatic tumour; if you see one lesion, look very carefully for any secondary lesions.

MRI

The most common image that you are likely to see in your exams is an MRI of the spine. This is because it is the best modality for looking at soft tissue in this region, and in clinical practice we use such scans for investigation of important pathology such as cauda equina syndrome.

When looking at the MRI, remember that T2 weighting has the liquid as white (often remembered by students as the shiny liquid metal robot in the movie *Terminator 2*), and therefore in T1 weighting the liquids are dark.

Orientate yourself by looking at the vertebral bodies. While you are doing this, you can assess them for even spacing and consistent intervertebral disc space.

Assess the spinal canal and cord for any signs of impingement.

Typical pathologies in finals include disc prolapse, tumour or vertebral body collapse.

Learning resources

On the wards

The ward environment provides an excellent opportunity for seeing normality, and you can start by inspecting imaging of patients you have clerked. You can usefully correlate imaging with pathology; for example, after finding coarse crepitations in the right base of a respiratory patient, you may see an area of shadowing. You can also do the converse, and ask doctors for any positive signs on imaging. You can then examine these patients and try to locate the signs which you expect to find.

> Be careful about changing clinical circumstances – it is no good listening for a florid pleural effusion which you have seen on radiograph, if it has been drained since!

Radiology meetings

Hospitals you are attached to will often have radiology department meetings which can be very useful learning opportunities. If you are looking for CT imaging, surgical meetings are often your best bet as intra-abdominal surgery is often guided by CT or MRI.

Hints and tips for radiology meetings:

1 Come well prepared. Radiologists and other doctors may be willing to slow the pace a little to teach you, but in busy hospital departments you should be prepared for a blitz through the images in a business-like fashion. You will gain very little if you are not already familiar with the normal.

2 If you get the chance, ask to present a case or patient, take a deep breath and be as systematic as you can. Take into account the feedback of the doctors, and try to act positively on any criticisms they have.

3 There may be other learning opportunities in hospitals, such as orthopaedics clinics and emergency departments. In particular, the minor injuries section of emergency departments will see a lot of normal and pathological radiographs, and is another area where you can see more peripheral radiography such as broken fingers, dislocated shoulders, fractured malleoli and so on. Ask both doctors and emergency nurse practitioners if they have any good cases and whether they can let you correlate the images with history and examination from their patients. Again, please be sensitive to the department's levels of patient demand, and plan your learning accordingly.

The internet

There are vast numbers of websites which are created by keen radiologists, for teaching their own trainees as well as medical students. However, even a simple Google Images search will produce any number of variable quality X-rays and other images. As with any open-source utility, be careful with what you are seeing, whether or not the images have been altered, and do not necessarily believe the label of the disease associated with the image. However, treated with due caution, the internet is a potentially endless supply for your imaging learning needs.

ECG

ECGs are snapshots of the electrical activity of the heart, and are therefore included under the imaging chapter. Furthermore, several of the principles you will take from this chapter can be aptly applied to ECGs – none more so than the principle of normality. Getting used to the plethora of normal variants can take even longer than X-rays as you are looking at many different views of the heart.

Cardiology ward rounds can be particularly useful. Many patients being seen will also require regular ECGs. If you are lucky, hovering around when ECGs are being looked at may get you 'volunteered' to interpret and present your finding, which is an invaluable opportunity to perform under pressure.

Emergency departments are also a useful area to learn about ECGs. All patients with chest pain should have a baseline ECG, and doctors will often be asked to look for any abnormalities which necessitate immediate treatment. Pay particular attention to the ECGs that doctors clear as normal, which should give you an idea of the variety of ECGs within the spectrum.

As with all investigations in this chapter, a systematic review of ECGs is vitally important, and should include all of the following areas:

- rate;
- rhythm;
- cardiac axis;
- presence of P waves;
- PR interval;
- ST segments;
- QT interval;
- T waves.

For medical finals, we particularly draw your attention to the following common pathologies:

- MI;
- PE;
- Tachyarrythmias;
- Bradyarrythmias;
- Long QT syndrome.

You should be able to identify the following patterns:

1 ST elevation or depression with or without T wave inversion;

2 'S1 Q3 T3' for PE;

3 first-, second- and third-degree heart block;

4 Torsade de Pointes;

5 VF/VT;

6 axis deviation.

Supplement your academic learning of ECGs and their pathologies with on-the-ward experience; this will allow you to practise performance under pressure, and force you to rapidly assess a 12-lead ECG. It also gives you exposure to a range of normal patients.

Presenting imaging

Presenting the results of an investigation is relatively straightforward if you have a system, and there is the potential to score highly if you present in a concise, structured and relevant manner.

Try to front load the answer if possible, eg if you know there is a clear abnormality, then tell the examiner early, and include some more advanced material to make it a distinction answer. This is in contrast to the examiner being forced to drag the answer out of you, or you infuriating them by going through a long-winded approach, finally ending up with a very mediocre answer, having told them a lot of unnecessary information.

Think:

- 'Why am I being presented with this investigation?' The odds are that it is *not* normal – examiners go to great lengths to find interesting or unusual cases for exams.

- 'How can I impress the examiners and stand out from the crowd?' Think of complications, causes, interesting facts that are either visible or that you would like to find out through history, examination or further investigations.

- 'Do I need a further investigation?' Think of the following:

  - Second radiograph of a different view if given a radiograph of a fracture ('One view is a view too few');
  - Chest radiograph if shown an abnormal ABG;
  - Rhythm strip if shown an ECG with an arrhythmia;
  - Echocardiography if shown an abnormal ECG or hear an abnormal heart sound;
  - Diagnostic aspiration, CT or bronchoscopy if shown an abnormal chest radiograph.

'What is the context of the XR/CT/ECG/ABG, and what are the most common abnormalities I could expect to find?' Look and you will see them!

Example: CXR of a pneumothorax

Methodical approach:

- This is a PA chest radiograph of Mr X.

- The alignment, penetration and rotation are within normal limits.

Then use a system to go through the CXR in a structured manner, commenting on lung fields, trachea, hilum and cardiac shadow to describe the radiograph.

Front-loaded answer:

- The most striking abnormality is a right-sided pneumothorax with approximately a 2 cm gap between the lung edge and chest wall.

- The trachea and mediastinum are central and there is no sign of tension pneumothorax.

- I would like to examine the patient for signs of distress and take a history of respiratory conditions such as COPD or asthma.

The answer spares the examiner the pain of waiting for the diagnosis, and allows you to demonstrate that you can not only spot the abnormality but can also appreciate the potential complications and understand the possible options regarding management. Any further questions from the examiner are now aimed at calculating whether you are a merit/distinction candidate. The only note of caution is to ask your colleagues from previous years if there are any particular styles of presentation that the examiners at your particular medical school prefer. You should try to find out if they always prefer you to start with an introductory paragraph with the patient's details and comments about the quality of the film.

Note that if you cannot spot any abnormality within the first few seconds, then your default position is to start describing the CXR using a system which covers the main structures visualized. If at some point during this methodical approach you spot the glaring abnormality, then you can present and discuss it.

Take a few seconds to use the clinical scenario and your wide-angle lens to rapidly spot the major abnormality. Once identified, keep alert for further associated abnormalities and think of the clinical significance of what you have found.

If you are truly struggling to see any pathology, then try the following:

● Think back to the clinical context in which this CXR was presented to you. It is highly likely that the pathology will relate to the presentation. For example:
  – Breathless with infective symptoms – consolidation, effusion, empyaema;
  – Breathless and wheeze – hyperexpanded lung fields with or without consolidation, pulmonary oedema;
  – Chest pain, breathlessness and peripheral oedema – pulmonary oedema;
  – Sudden-onset breathlessness with pleuritic chest pain – subtle lung edge of pneumothorax, or if truly normal, consider pulmonary embolus.

● In the stress of finals the temptation is to rush everything you do. With CXR interpretation this manifests as a student peering as closely as possible at the image in order to somehow zoom in or better visualize pathology. This is generally to be avoided, as the majority of findings are more clearly seen when you stand back and have a better appreciation of the overall film.

● Consider commonly missed areas, which include under the diaphragm, behind the heart, in the apices, in the soft tissues and along the ribs.

> Begin every examination of a CXR as you would a patient, and inspect from a distance before moving closer. Most pathology presented to you in finals will be immediately obvious if you stand back and think about the clinical scenario.

Example: ECG of fast atrial fibrillation

Methodical approach:

● This is an ECG of...

● The rate is approximately...

● No P waves are seen, and the ventricular rate is approximately 170/min.

● There are no TW or ST abnormalities.

● I think this is an ECG showing atrial fibrillation at a rate of 170.

Front-loading approach:

- This is an ECG of...

- The most striking abnormality is atrial fibrillation with a ventricular rate of approximately 170 beats per minute and no ischaemic changes.

- I would like to know the blood pressure, GCS and if there is any degree of breathlessness or chest pain.

Again the difference is that while the structured approach offers more information, the examiner is not really interested in most of it. There are a lot more marks to be gained with the second approach, which shows the examiner that not only can you identify the abnormality but you also know how to recognize the compromised patient, as this would necessitate emergency treatment.

As with CXRs, it is important to have a system to fall back on if you do not see anything immediately obvious in your initial scan of the ECG. This could be in any form that you feel comfortable, but a common method is to appraise the rhythm strip looking for arrhythmias or block, then look at the ST and T waves for signs of ischaemia or infarction. Don't forget the clinical scenario given, as shown below:

- Middle-aged male presents with heavy central chest pain radiating down his left arm and sweating profusely – look for ST elevation or depression in the leads representing the inferior, anterior, lateral and posterior regions of the heart.

- Young patient presents with lightheadness and palpitations – look for a supraventricular tachycardia.

- Elderly patient with fever, cough, sputum and breathlessness becomes lightheaded and hypotensive – look for new onset atrial fibrillation.

- Female with family history of PE or recent immobility presents with breathlessness and right-sided pleuritic chest pain – sinus tachycardia, new atrial fibrillation, or right heart strain, ie findings associated with a pulmonary embolus.

Example: arterial blood gas

Case A: elderly patient presenting generally unwell. Methodical approach:

- The pH shows an acidosis.

- The pCO_2 is low, with a normal pO_2.

- The base excess is negative and there is a raised lactate.

- I think there is a metabolic acidosis with respiratory compensation.

Front-loading approach:

- There is a metabolic acidosis associated with a raised lactate and the patient has respiratory compensation.
- The other values, including glucose, haemoglobin, calcium and electrolytes are within normal.
- Common causes of a lactic acidosis include sepsis and shock.
- A lactate of greater than 5 in the acute setting carries a raised mortality.

Case B: arterial blood gas of a patient presenting with an acute exacerbation of COPD. Methodical approach:

- The patient is acidotic.
- The patient is hypoxic with an elevated pCO_2.
- The bicarbonate is elevated and the lactate is normal.
- I think this patient has type 2 respiratory failure and is acidotic.

Front-loading approach:

- The patient has type 2 respiratory failure and is acidotic.
- There is some metabolic compensation, with a high bicarbonate showing that they are likely to be a chronic CO_2 retainer and that this is an acute on chronic deterioration.
- They should be treated with maximal medical therapy, a blood gas repeated in 30 minutes, and if they remain acidotic BIPAP non-invasive ventilation should be considered as long as there are no contraindications such as a pneumothorax.

Example: CT head

Case A. Extradural haemorrhage. Methodical approach:

- The cranial vault appears to be intact.
- There is no midline shift.
- There is a high attenuation lesion on anterior aspect of the right side of the brain.
- It appears to be lenticular in shape, with a prominent middle and thin edges.

- I would characterize this as an extradural bleed in the right frontoparietal region, which is typically caused by trauma to the side of the head, and rupture of the middle meningeal artery, which lies underneath the temporal bone.

- The patient may have a history of trauma, and may need neurosurgical intervention.

Front-loading approach:

- This patient has an extradural haemorrhage, presenting as a lenticular area of high attenuation on the right frontoparietal region of the brain.

- This is most likely due to trauma of the middle meningeal branch of the external carotid artery.

- There is no associated midline shift, but this patient may need neurosurgical input.

- The cranial vault is intact.

- There are no other abnormalities within the brain matter.

Case B. Subdural haemorrhage. Methodical approach:

- The cranial vault is intact.

- There is significant midline shift to the right, with ventricular compression.

- There is a semi-lunar region of high attention on the left parietal region of the brain.

- There are no other abnormalities within the brain matter.

- This appearance is consistent with a subdural haemorrhage, caused by rupture of the bridging veins.

- This patient will need neurosurgical input, and consideration for evacuation of the haematoma.

Front-loading approach:

- This patient has a subdural haemorrhage presenting as a semi-lunar area of high attenuation on the left parietal region.

- This is accompanied by significant midline shift as seen in the ventricular system, and therefore represents a neurosurgical emergency as this patient is now at risk of coning through the foramen magnum and central respiratory depression. The treatment for this would be a prompt decompression of the heamatoma, possibly through a burr hole.

- In systematic review, the cranial vault is intact, and there are no other areas of abnormal attenuation apart from some minor calcification in the chorioid plexus. This might be due to old age, and this might also explain why the patient was at risk of a subdural haemorrhage as age-related brain atrophy may have stretched their bridging veins.

PITFALLS

- If you don't actually know what is going on, then it is difficult (but not impossible) to give a front-loaded answer.

- In such cases where you have a collection of abnormalities but are unable to draw them together it is nevertheless important to let the examiner know that you have identified the key points, and then you can either volunteer a few differentials or be helped along by the examiner, who, happy that you have found the abnormalities, is a little better-disposed towards helping you reach the correct diagnosis.

Summary

- Think of the case being discussed when you are shown an investigation. The odds are in favour of it showing a common pathological finding or complication of the condition.

- Your wide-angle lens should be used to enable you to carry out pattern recognition from a distance before you go closer to scrutinize the detail.

- Give yourself a few seconds of silence to spot the abnormality, and then start to describe your findings while thinking about the clinical significance of what you have found.

- If you spot an abnormality early, don't forget to look for others.

- If there is clearly one main finding, then provide a front-loaded answer and think about any interesting points of discussion.

- If you are unable to find any abnormality after about five seconds, you should start to describe what you see using a standard system.

- Practise your pattern recognition using CXR, ECG, ABG and CT examples aiming to spot the major abnormality within about five seconds.

PART THREE

Written examinations

CHAPTER 11

Memory audit and differential diagnosis trees

How to use this chapter

Many students find that their memory does not always behave as they would like it to, and therefore techniques to enhance the amount of retained information are most valuable. Whereas the sample curriculum indicates what you should know, this chapter deals with what you do and do not actually know. This process starts with assessment known as the memory audit, and allows you to establish what remains to be covered, or what you have already forgotten. Another technique which we describe is the construction of differential diagnosis trees, which test your ability to recall information in a systematic manner.

Memory audit

In clinical practice, we audit our performance against a gold standard, note any deviations and attempt to correct them. We can borrow the principles of this for our revision, and a memory audit can help to guide how you spend your time, as well as being a revision exercise in itself. We will discuss how to construct a gold standard template, and then how to use it.

Gold standard template construction

The **sample curriculum** in Chapter 13 should give you an idea of what you need to learn in order to pass finals; the next step is to source that data. Use books which we recommend in Chapter 14, as well as your own notes, lecture materials and information gleaned from teaching sessions.

Once you have this material to hand, organizing it in a fashion that you can make best use of is critical, both for revision and for audit. We have therefore included below another useful tool for your revision: a 'gold standard template'. This can be filled out for each and every condition, covering the main areas of knowledge needed for finals. To find out exactly how much depth is required in it you should refer to the sample curriculum.

If you have a gold standard template, you will be able to check your own performance against the required standard, by direct comparison between what you can recall and what you should be able to recall. In reality, there is no such thing as having 'finished' learning about a topic – your MI gold standard template may be different from that of a medical registrar, which may be different still from a cardiology consultant's.

The key is that you aim to construct a template at the level at which your standard of knowledge is required, eg for passing medical finals. You can refer back to the sample curriculum for further details on this. There may be a difference between distinction-level templates, which may include more evidence-based data, rare conditions, in-depth pathology and physiology.

The construction of a gold standard template is a useful exercise in and of itself. You will be required to source, read, understand and organize information about clinical conditions in a stratified and systematic manner.

There may be recommended reading from your medical school which is an indicator of an appropriate level of knowledge. You can also compare with peers to see that your standard is not a huge outlier in terms of being too much or too little, compared to your examining cohort. There are also several common-sense considerations. For example, using a large medical reference text may be appropriate and sufficient, whereas undertaking a literature search or using several specialist cardiology textbooks may be more than the level required. You may, however, wish to consider these options if you attempt to construct a distinction level template.

The memory audit template is also free to download from http://www.koganpage.com/editions/how-to-master-your-medical-school-finals/9780749463533.

Memory audit template

Introduction

Basic description of the disease.

Epidemiology

i)   UK incidence : /100,000 (or common, uncommon, rare)

ii)   Male : female ratio:

iii)   Risk factors:

–

–

–

Pathology

Mechanism of disease:
    Genetics:

Presentation

Symptoms and signs:

i)

ii)

iii)

iv)

Specific history questions:

i)

ii)

Investigations

i)

ii)

iii)

iv)

v)

Differential diagnoses

i)

ii)

iii)

iv)

Management

i)

ii)

iii)

iv)

v)

Complications and prognosis

i)

ii)

iii)

iv)

v)

Example completed template

Medical template: myocardial infarction.

Introduction

Infarction of an area of cardiac tissue due to the interruption of the blood supply delivered by the coronary arteries. Usually due to thrombosis following the rupture of an atheromatous plaque, with other causes including spasm of the vessel or vasculitis.

Pathology

Coronary arteries

Immediately after the aortic valve, from the left and right coronary sinuses:

Left main coronary artery –> left anterior descending + left circumflex.

LAD runs in the anterior interventricular groove, supplying the anterior septum, anterior left ventricular wall, and the apex.

LCX runs in the left atrio-ventricular groove, supplying the left atrium and posterior, lateral and inferior left ventricle.

Right coronary artery runs in the right atrio-ventricular groove, supplying the right atrium, ventricle and the infero-posterior left ventricle.

Right posterior artery runs in the inter-ventricular groove, and supplies the posterior aspect of the heart.

The RCA supplies the SA node in 60% and the AV node in 90%, therefore MI can lead to sinus bradycardia and AV block.

i) UK incidence: 450/100,000

ii) Male : female ratio: Male > female

Risk factors:

i) Age

ii) Sex

iii) FH of IHD

iv) Smoking

v) Hypertension

vi) Diabetes mellitus

vii) Hyperlipidaemia/hypercholestrolaemia

viii) Obesity

ix) Sedentary lifestyle

x) Cocaine abuse

xi) Left ventricular hypertrophy

xii) Chlamydia bacteraemia

Genetics

Complex inheritance

Presentation

Symptoms:

i) Chest pain – retrosternal, sudden onset, crushing, radiating to jaw + down left arm, associated with dyspnoea, palpitations, nausea and sweating, constant > 20 mins, exacerbated by exertion, severe

ii) Dyspnoea

iii) Nausea

iv) Palpitations

v) Syncope

Can present as silent MI – syncope, pulmonary oedema, vomiting, confusion.
Can present as jaw or tooth pain (less commonly).

Signs:

i) Pallor, sweating, distress

ii) Heart failure signs, eg JVP, basal creps

iii) Tachycardia or bradycardia

iv) 4th heart sound

Specific history questions

i)   Any history of heart disease in the family?

ii) Any previous episodes?

iii) Was it on exertion or at rest?

Investigations

i)   Bloods – FBC, U+E, CK/Troponin T+I

ii) ECG – pathological Q waves, ST elevation, T wave inversion

iii) CXR

iv) Coronary angiography

v)   Echo

Differential diagnoses

i)   Angina

ii) Aortic dissection

iii) Pericarditis

iv) Myocarditis

v)   PE

vi) GORD

Management

i)   ABCDE, IV access + oxygen

ii) 300 mg aspirin PO (chewed) and 300 mg clopidogrel

iii) Analgesia – morphine 5–10 mg + metoclopramide 10 mg IV

iv) GTN spray/tablet sublingual

v)   If indicated, percutaneous coronary intervention (PCI)

vi) Thrombolysis – streptokinase 1.5 million units in 100 ml saline in 1 hour or rt-PA (Alteplase) if already used streptokinase > 4 days ago, Tenecteplase – 500 ug/kg bolus

vii) Beta blocker – atenolol 5 mg IV

Complications

In order of frequency:

i) Arrhythmias – sick sinus, brady or tachy

ii) Cardiac failure

iii) Mitral valve prolapse due to papillary muscle rupture

iv) Rupture +/– tamponade

v) Ventricular septal defect

vi) Mural thrombus → stroke

vii) Dressler's syndrome: autoimmune pericarditis

Prognosis

The prognosis in myocardial infarction is intimately linked to the treatments given, whether the patient is treated in a timely fashion, whether they suffer any complications, and what these complications are. ACE inhibitors can influence survival rate post MI, by a mechanism that is thought to involve remodelling of the myocardium.

Advantages and disadvantages of memory audit

This type of auditing can play an important role in directing your revision towards areas in which you are deficient or less competent.

It encourages a comprehensive overview of a topic, symptom or organ system. Limitations:

● You will only be able to identify gaps in your knowledge if you are aware of their existence. Therefore having carefully constructed gold standard templates, or having a reliable resource to compare to, is a prerequisite for undertaking audits.

● It is a diagnostic test for yourself and will require reading and note making as a follow-up for each time you do it.

Differential diagnosis trees

Many students spend the majority of their time on the input side of learning, but practising the output is often neglected. There are a number of output activities which you can undertake, such as practice MCQ questions, and simulations as described in previous chapters. However, another more general form of output practice is differential diagnosis tree construction.

This method of revision can be undertaken anywhere with no resources, and is a fantastic way of making use of downtime. It can be triggered by events which you have seen on the ward; for example, if you clerk a patient presenting with a particular sign or symptom, this can prompt a lunchtime or evening differential diagnosis tree session in order to help your revision.

How it works

Step 1. Take a condition or symptom.

Step 2. Write down all the differential diagnoses which can explain this symptom; this is your **branch**.

Step 3. Pick a branch, and write down the information you know about that condition.

Step 4. List the information which you do not know or are not sure of, for that branch.

Step 5. Once that branch is exhausted, move on to the next one.

Step 6. At the end, check your branches against a book or notes to see what else you have missed.

Step 7. Read over the lists of information you didn't not know, and revise it.

Below is a worked example of this.

Example differential diagnosis tree

Step 1. Take a symptom from a patient you have seen. This example tree was triggered after seeing a patient with chest pain.

Step 2. Create your branches:

- Chest wall:
    - Musculoskeletal pain rib fracture (movement, sharp, previous trauma)
    - Herpes zoster
- Lung:
    - Pneumonia
    - Pulmonary embolus
    - Pleural irritation

- Nearby organs:

  — Gastritis

  — Gastro-oesophageal reflux disease

  — Hepatitis

- Cardiac causes:

  — Myocardial infarction

  — Acute coronary syndrome

  — Pericardial effusion

This forms the 'branches' of your chest pain differential diagnosis tree.

Step 3. Branch analysis. Pick a branch (in this case, MI), and list the things which you know:

- MI.

  — Signs and symptoms – SOB + chest pain, autonomic features, can be silent in elderly.

  — Basic pathology – atherosclerosis in coronary vessels. Risk factors – smoking, male sex, diabetes mellitus, hypercholesterolaemia, FH. Can also be associated with vasospasm of vessels.

  — Management – anticoagulant (aspirin 300 mg if non-allergic) + oxygen, morphine not generally agreed currently and anti-emetic.

  — Consider for PCI

  — Complications – early: sudden death; rupture of vessel wall +/– haemopericardium + tamponade (? Treatment = pericardiocentesis); late: valvular incompetence; Dressler's syndrome; CCF.

Step 4. List the things which you don't know or you are not sure about:

- Indications for PCI.

- ECG interpretation.

- Coronary artery distribution and supply of myocardium.

- Pericardiocentesis.

Step 5. Move on to each branch; you may stick with other cardiac diagnoses, or go on to cover pneumonia or PE.

KEY POINT

Remember that this exercise is for you to use; don't feel obliged to finish every branch of every tree! Use as much time as you have available which you would otherwise be 'wasting'.

Advantages and disadvantages of DDT construction as a form of revision

Advantages:

- A DDX tree can be done anywhere with a simple pen and paper.

- It is a problem-solving approach.

- It can be stimulated by clinical scenarios, as well as reading or peer questioning.

- It is a great way to use downtime while waiting in a queue, outside a clinic or anywhere!

Disadvantages:

- It is not as systematic as an audit, which follows a rigid structure.

- If you have a poor baseline knowledge, you will benefit less from DDT.

Ensure you keep your DDTs, and check them for content when you get the chance in the library or at home.

Using DDTs has really helped me to use my spare time to sit and work on medical revision material. It's great!

JL, Liverpool University undergraduate

Summary

- Memory audit is a method of assessing your own revision needs.

- It is also a useful form of revision in and of itself.

- The sample curriculum (Chapter 13) is specifically designed for this type of memory audit.

- Use our sample templates to help you take a systematic approach.

- Differential diagnosis trees are a technique to consolidate information.

- This can be useful in downtime, or when triggered by seeing patients on the ward.

CHAPTER 12

Revising for MCQ and EMQ examinations

How to use this chapter

Revising medical concepts and facts is a very different prospect from preparing for MCQs. The particular examination format is limited, particularly by having a requirement of similar answers to offer. EMQs can vary more in terms of answer stems, but again are fairly constrained. This chapter looks at the specific limitations of the examination to highlight how to take advantage of specific revision for written examinations to increase performance.

Question spotting

Spotting questions seems a cynical way to revise for finals; after all, shouldn't we be interested in a fully rounded revision performance, leaving no stone unturned in our pursuit of knowledge? The honest answer for many of us is probably yes. However, a good multiple-choice test is much like that first week on the job: it makes you realize how little we actually know. Dealing with uncertainty is part and parcel of a career in medicine, and increasing your performance in finals by focusing on certain commonly recurring themes may allow you to score higher than your overall knowledge base would suggest. Having said that, this is not a procedure you should base your final year upon; other activities such as history taking, ward experience and memory audit are much more rounded and provide the backbone of your knowledge base.

Question spotting is reserved for that extra performance in the technique of approaching your final examinations.

Asking seniors

Asking final-year students what came up in their exams is a great potential resource. In particular, you can ask them for any questions they found difficult or unusual – and this will give you at least an indicator of what you might need to read up on and what might be popular with examiners. The best time to do this will be after their finals exam, as their memory will be most fresh. Be polite and remember that they are doing you a favour, not performing a duty; be understanding if they are tired and don't want to post-mortem a recently traumatic experience.

Macro analysis

The composition of the material set in your exam may follow a particular distribution at your medical school. It is important to tailor your revision to the material which your MCQs will be based upon. Read past papers, ask seniors, and refer to curriculum documentation to decipher the percentages.

In the first instance, it is therefore optimal to follow a pattern of revision which matches this distribution as it will maximize your overall marks. This phenomenon occurs because of the principle of diminishing returns, which states that the initial marks for each sub-topic are the easiest to obtain, but it becomes increasingly harder to improve your score, the higher it gets. So if you increase the time you spend on surgery from 10 to 100 hours, you might increase your marks significantly. However, if you increase it from 100 to 200, you might find that increase less significant, and those extra hours might be better spent on, for example, ENT, O&G and microbiology.

Similar conditions and their discriminators

The process of answering MCQs involves looking at a clinical situation and identifying a disease, treatment, symptom or complication from the stem. However, there are certain rules or limitations which examiners must abide by in order to set effective MCQ questions, and once you know these rules, you can exploit them through targeted revision and preparation.

First, MCQs have to have multiple answers which offer a reasonable alternative to the actual answer. This is because the process of MCQ question creation forces examiners to reveal the answer on the paper, and then disguise it amongst a crowd.

The selection of the correct answer will be on one (or less commonly, multiple) dis-criminators. How can we use this limitation in our revision? Clearly, it is easier to set questions on conditions for which there are multiple similar diagnoses. Take the symptom of a 'headache', for example. This has a large list of possible causes, each of which can be separated by risk factors, onset, character, subsidiary symptoms, etc. Therefore, if we take the symptom of headache and look, we can construct a chart of the possibilities stratified by each of these factors.

Revising in this way has a focus on similar conditions, and lists the fine dif-ferences between them, which is exactly the type of skill you will need in the MCQ test. This kind of activity will give a very high yield for MCQ exams, and direct you towards the more commonly or easily questioned topics within each specialty.

Another method of discriminating answers is to ask a quantitative question: which condition is more or less likely? It is therefore important to attach a frequency or probability to your knowledge of diseases, and attach a first-line or second-line fre-quency to treatments. This will allow you to pick the best answer from a batch. How can we then prepare for this? It is important to have a good understanding of relative frequencies in terms of how often they occur, and in particular to which demographic groups. For example, abdominal pain and cramping with diarrhoea in someone below the age of 30 is more likely to be ulcerative colitis than in an elderly person. However, in the elderly person, diverticular disease is more likely.

This information is often not listed in books in this manner – 'What are the most likely diseases for this presentation in this type of patient' – but this is how you will be tested in these probability-discriminated MCQ questions. Therefore, in preparation for this type of examination, creating a differential list based on probability gives you a wonderful resource to answer questions with. You may need to list many options, and be careful to arrange them in a fixed order of frequency, either ascending or descending.

Good or bad guesser?

Students often say that they are able to narrow down to a choice of two options, and that they then have to make an educated guess. Students are sometimes advised to see whether or not they are a good 'guesser' by conducting a study of whether or not their guesses in these circumstances are right. They are then advised to pick the one they think is correct if they are 'good guessers', or to actively pick the option they think is incorrect if they are 'bad guessers'. We do not recommend this approach as it is fraught with several problems; first there is the risk of interference with your normal answering process, in that picking the 'wrong' answer may influence how you identify the correct answers in the first place. Second and most important, there is enough noise in the data for even very robust studies of your performance to be wrong. For example, if you flip a coin 1,000 times and get 550 heads, should you pick heads the next time? Avoid this kind of technique and try to focus on how to discriminate between answers by thorough revision of the material.

How to use practice MCQs

> I practised hundreds of online MCQs and still did poorly in my mock
> exam – what am I doing wrong?
>
> PW, final-year medical student

This is a common problem faced by students who blindly undertake high volumes of MCQs without making the most of them.

Start by using multiple sources of MCQs, to ensure you are covering the variety, depth and breadth of questions for medical school finals. Online databanks, question books and medical school past papers from both your own university and others are invaluable resources to practise with.

It is easy and tempting to bash through a large set of questions, and then look up the answers in a tick-the-box exercise. However, we recommend that you reduce this pace significantly to get the most out of your MCQ practice. Do smaller groups of practice questions – 10–20 at a time. After each batch, go back and check your answers, and hopefully the thought processes that got you to your answer will still be fresh in your mind. Note down the incorrect answers, and once you collate the results from your practice, try to assess whether your knowledge in that area is sufficient. You can refer to the sample curriculum in Chapter 13 for guidance. If the question was about viral causes of myocarditis, do not just write down the cause that was listed in the MCQ. You need to ensure that you know the other viral causes, and the other non-viral causes, of myocarditis.

This method is slower and more intense, and in some ways takes out the relaxing part of the MCQ practice. However, you will get far more from the material, and retain it for longer. Note in particular:

- Commonly recurring conditions;

- Commonly recurring questions.

You may be able to gain easy marks from a question you have tackled before, and these small percentages could turn a fail into a pass for students who are near the borderline. Keep a careful note of these when they occur; this may be particularly easy to do if you are doing questions electronically. Team up with a group of friends and share your findings on common topics and questions; this will allow you to get maximum benefit for minimum effort.

Trigger words

Here is a guide to some trigger words that would indicate certain things, eg cricket-ball impact with epidural haemorrhage.
   Cardiovascular:

   Stokes–Adams attack – 'sudden' loss of consciousness, no warning, pallor during episode, flushing and rapid return of full consciousness.

   Infective endocarditis – generally unwell (febrile, lethargy, weight loss) with clubbing, splenomegaly, new murmur.

Respiratory:

   Asthma – nocturnal cough.

   Pneumothorax – tall thin male, smoker.

   PE – chest pain and breathlessness in young female, eg on oral contraceptive, two weeks postop, long flight, malignancy.

Neurology:

   SAH – sudden onset occipital headache, 'like being hit with a bat or struck'.

   EDH – cricket-ball impact, initial lucid period and subsequent drowsiness.

   Meningitis – febrile, nonspecifically unwell initially then later neck ache, stiffness, photophobic.

   Temporal arteritis – jaw ache, scalp tenderness with headache.

   TIA – visual loss 'like a curtain descending'.

   MS – different episodes over time, different each time, eg painful eye movements, arm numbness, unsteadiness.

   Myasthenia gravis – weakness towards the end of the day.

Statistically inaccurate representation

In medical finals certain questions occur more frequently in MCQs than they do in real life. This is partly because some conditions are difficult to find patients for, and in practice may only be seen by specialists on a few occasions each year. Futhermore, the OSCE examinations will feature more of the 'mainstream' material in terms of physical findings as the questions the examiner may ask, and therefore the written examination is a good place to test more esoteric knowledge. Be particularly aware of the following conditions:

Cardiology – cardiac myopathies, pericarditis;

Respiratory – Endocrine-secreting tumours, sarcoidosis;

Neurology – Waterhouse–Friderichsen syndrome, Guillain Barre syndrome;

Rheumatology – Behcet's disease, Marfan's syndrome;

Gastroenterology – Gilbert's syndrome, primary sclerosing cholangitis, primary biliary sclerosis, autoimmune hepatitis, inflammatory bowel disease, coeliac disease;

Endocrinology – Acromegaly, Cushing's syndrome, Addison's syndrome;

Paediatrics – HSP, cystic fibrosis, muscular dystrophy.

Look out for these conditions, particularly when answering MCQs on these particular subspecialties.

Summary

- Starting revision very early on for MCQs can yield excellent results as you have plenty of time to prepare specifically for them (most students leave it until too late).

- Revise MCQs in parallel to your main revision, rather than tacking this on at the end in the final month.

- Undertaking question spotting can be a very valuable experience and increase performance.

- Remember to do a macro analysis at the start and in the middle of your six months to ensure you are spending the appropriate amount of time on revising each subtopic.

- Look out for trigger words and statistically inaccurate representations.

- Do not attempt to play the guessing game; focus on aiming for informed guesses, at the worst.

CHAPTER 13

The sample curriculum

How to use this chapter

Students often complain about not knowing the depth to which they should know the vast material required for medical school finals. The sample curriculum is an immensely useful tool which lists the core topics and gives an indication of how much detail will be expected of you. It is set up in a table format, with tick boxes for you to fill in for your own 'audit of knowledge' purposes.

> I never know how much I need to know, and because of this I'm anxious and overworked all the time!
>
> AB, Liverpool University

What is a sample curriculum?

Any sample curriculum should reflect the final body of knowledge which fresh graduate doctors are required to have. The sources for this data include the foundation curriculum which is used to judge the performance of first-year junior doctors, a consensus from medical school graduates and examining consultants. We have also based this device upon the learning objectives of the medical schools where we teach medical finals students. These represent two very different courses, one of which is a PBL-based course, and the other a traditional, lecture-based course, to produce the list of conditions and their depth. We have also drawn upon the foundation curriculum, which indicates what you will be expected to know in the year after you graduate, and furthermore worked closely with core medical and surgical references we used in our own preparation for finals, which are listed in Chapter 14. We have also consulted with a range of recent graduates from many medical schools to give an up-to-date and practical guide to what is represented in medical school finals. This document represents a unique tool that has been created from reliable and important sources for medical school finals and united into one single document.

As with any attempt to summarize the required knowledge for finals, there may be regional variations. Individual specialist consultants may wish or demand that you know more about a certain topic while you are on your clinical attachment. We have tried to take a step back, gather information from multiple different sources, and condense this information into a student-friendly resource that facilitates learning processes such as memory audit (see Chapter 11).

You may find critics of individual points in the curriculum. We advise you that if in doubt, cover more rather than less.

Nevertheless, we hope that you find our curriculum a useful, thorough device for guiding your revision.

Although we cannot guarantee that every student in every medical school will require the same information, this curriculum has drawn on all of these sources to produce a reasonable reflection of the pass requirements from a variety of UK medical schools. We have created it with the sole purpose of helping you assess your own level of knowledge, and our intention is for it to serve as highly valuable document in your revision for finals.

It is presented as a large table which lists the key conditions under each category (medicine, cardiac, respiratory, etc). Critically, it also gives an explanation as to the depth of knowledge you should have to pass medical school finals, using a system described below.

Format

The curriculum is set out as a table which has the key diseases for each specialty and a label for each of the following:

Epidemiology and aetiology;

Pathology;

Signs and symptoms;

Investigations and differential diagnoses;

Management;

Prognosis and complications.

Under each category, there is an indicator as to the depth of knowledge required. These fall into four categories: critical, important, moderate and superficial. These are further explained below.

Critical knowledge

This is a subject area which you must be intimately familiar with. If you have any gaps in this area you are at risk of failing, as well as becoming an unsafe practitioner. This information should be on the tip of your tongue and in the forefront of your mind.

Please note that critical and important knowledge categories require the same knowledge base, but for critical knowledge the recall time should be minimal, and you may be called upon to recall this information under pressure from examiners during situations such as in OSCEs. With 'important knowledge', you are more likely to be tested under conditions such as MCQs where you have more time to recall and apply it.

Important knowledge

This is a subject area with which you should be familiar and have a good understanding. This material is well represented in medical school finals, and gaps in this area will result in poor marks, with significant gaps putting you at risk of failing.

Epidemiology/aetiology. You should know whether the disease is common, uncommon or rare, and its relative frequency compared to differential diagnoses (this is especially important for MCQ questions; see Chapter 12 for further details). You should know the demographic characteristics of the disease, including age, sex and ethnic distribution. You should be aware of risk factors for the disease.

Signs and symptoms. You should know the presentation of the disease, what signs may be seen, and the relative frequency of these signs being present. You should know specific history questions pertaining to this condition, eg 'How many pillows do you sleep on?' for cardiac failure.

Investigations and differential diagnoses. You should know the required investigations and their likely outcome. You should have a good list of differential diagnoses and awareness of how to distinguish the conditions.

Management. You should know the conservative, medical and surgical manage-ments options. You should be aware of specific drugs and their doses, and the risks of the surgical procedures.

Complications and prognosis. You should know the complications that can occur including time frames (immediate, early and late). You should know the factors affecting prognosis, and which drugs affect the outcomes.

Moderate knowledge

This is a subject area which you should be grossly familiar with, but you may not require complete knowledge of all the subcategories of knowledge to the same depth as 'important knowledge'.

Epidemiology/aetiology. You should know whether the disease is common, uncommon or rare. You should know if there are any gender or ethnicity biases.

Pathology. You should know the basic mechanism of the disease, names of pathogens and associated genes. You may not need to know specific immuno-logical or molecular basis, or full detail on disease subtypes.

Signs and symptoms. You should be aware of the presentation of the disease, and they key points in the history which support the diagnosis.

Management. You should know the treatments available. You may not need to know specific doses or regimens (eg oncological chemotherapy, management of myasthaenia gravis).

Complications. You should be aware of the complications that can occur. You may not need a specific time frame for prognosis or complications, only a general idea of the outlook for the patient.

Superficial knowledge

You should have heard of this condition and know what causes it and how it presents. You may not need to know the full details of its investigation, management or complications for medical school finals.

Special notes/lists

Here we list miscellaneous information that is commonly useful for medical stu-dents. In particular, we detail the common 'need to know' lists that medical students are regularly asked on ward rounds or in examination settings, as well as any other miscellaneous information which is important but does not fall under the system we have devised.

How to use this device

Tips:

- This curriculum can be used by itself to assess your own level of knowledge, and to build up a picture of what is required in planning for your revision.

- We include more details of self-assessment of knowledge in Chapter 11, 'Memory audit and differential diagnosis trees'.

- As with any audit, you must compare yourself to a gold standard. This sample curriculum offers a standard of knowledge which allows you to make that comparison.

- It would be impossible to include all of the factual information required to pass finals in this book. You must refer to other resources such as recommended textbooks in Chapter 14 to find the appropriate information which you have identified by using the curriculum.

- However, this is also where the sample curriculum performs its second function: guiding your active revision. You may look at the cardiovascular section of a textbook with some degree of trepidation at its sheer depth, and not know what level to study to. Using this sample curriculum, you will be able to extract the relevant information, for example in-depth management and investigation of myocardial infarction, but with a far shorter time spent with cardiomyopathies looking for the key information listed in the curriculum (causes, recognition).

Sample curriculum key

Critical knowledge = (C)

Important knowledge = (I)

Moderate knowledge = (M)

Superficial knowledge = (S)

The medical sample curriculum

TABLE 13.1 The medical sample curriculum

1. Cardiac	Epidemiology/ aetiology	Pathology	Symptoms and signs	Investigation and DDX	Management	Complications and prognosis
1) Angina pectoris	I	I	C	C	C	I
2) Myocardial infarction	I	I	C	C	C	C
3) Aortic dissection	M	M	C	C	C	I
4) Pericarditis	M	S	I	I	M	M
5) Cardiac arrhythmias	I	M	I	I	I	I
6) Heart failure	M	I	I	I	C	I
7) Hypertension	I	M	M	I	I	I
8) Infective endocarditis	I	I	C	I	C	I
9) Cardiac myopathies	S	M	M	M	S	S
10) Congenital heart disease	M	M	M	M	M	M
11) Valvular disorders	I	C	C	I	I	I

Special notes:
ECG interpretation, management of acute heart failure, acute chest pain

Lists:
Causes of murmurs

2. Respiratory	Epidemiology/ aetiology	Pathology	Symptoms and signs	Investigation and DDX	Management	Complications and prognosis
1) Pulmonary embolism	C	I	C	I	I	I
2) Pneumonia	I	I	C	C	C	I
3) Pneumothorax	I	M	C	I	C	I
4) Asthma	I	M	I	I	C	I
5) COPD	I	M	I	I	I	I
6) Pleural effusion	I	C	I	C	I	I
7) Lung CA	I	I	I	I	I	I
8) Cystic fibrosis	M	I	I	I	I	M
9) Tuberculosis	M	M	M	M	I	I
10) Sarcoidosis	S	M	M	M	S	S
11) Bronchiectasis	M	I	I	I	I	I
12) Pulmonary fibrosis	I	I	M	M	M	M

Special notes:
X-ray interpretation
Peak flow
Spirometry
ARDS

Lists:
Causes of pleural effusion
Risk factors for PE
Types of pneumonia
Complications of lung cancer
Stages of tuberculosis
Types of pulmonary fibrosis which are apical and basal

TABLE 13.1 *Continued*

3. Endocrine	Epidemiology/ aetiology	Pathology	Symptoms and signs	Investigation and DDX	Management	Complications and prognosis
1) Diabetes + ketoacidosis	I ☐	I ☐	I ☐	I ☐	C ☐	C ☐
2) Thyroid disease	I ☐	M ☐	C ☐	I ☐	I ☐	I ☐
3) Parathyroid disease	M ☐	M ☐	I ☐	I ☐	I ☐	M ☐
4) Phaechromocytoma	S ☐	S ☐	S ☐	M ☐	M ☐	S ☐
5) Pituitary disease	M ☐	M ☐	I ☐	I ☐	M ☐	M ☐
6) Acromegaly	S ☐	M ☐	C ☐	I ☐	M ☐	M ☐
7) Cushing's syndrome	M ☐	I ☐	I ☐	I ☐	M ☐	M ☐
8) Addison's disease	M ☐	M ☐	I ☐	I ☐	M ☐	M ☐

Special notes:
Phaechromocytoma rule of 10%
Multiple endocrine neoplasia

Lists:
Causes of neck lumps
Serological testing of endocrine disorders, eg synacthen test, oral glucose tolerance test, dexamethasone suppression test
Complications of diabetes mellitus

4. Renal + urology	Epidemiology/ aetiology	Pathology	Symptoms and signs	Investigation and DDX	Management	Complications and prognosis
1) Acute renal failure	M	I	I	I	C	C
2) Chronic renal failure, transplantation, treatment	M	I	I	I	I	I
3) UTI + pyelonephritis	I	M	I	I	M	I
4) Haematuria	M	I	I	I	I	I
5) Urinary retention	I	M	I	M	I	M
6) PKD	M	M	M	S	M	M
7) Renal cell carcinoma	S	M	M	M	M	M

Special notes:
Indications for dialysis, look for renal transplant patients in medical OSCEs
Nephrotic syndrome

Lists:
Causes of acute and chronic renal failure

TABLE 13.1 *Continued*

5. Gastrointestinal	Epidemiology/ aetiology	Pathology	Symptoms and signs	Investigation and DDX	Management	Complications and prognosis
1) Upper GI bleed	I ☐	I ☐	C ☐	I ☐	C ☐	I ☐
2) Peptic ulcer	I ☐	M ☐	I ☐	I ☐	I ☐	I ☐
3) Malignancy	I ☐	I ☐	I ☐	I ☐	M ☐	I ☐
4) Dysphagia	C ☐	M ☐	C ☐	M ☐	M ☐	M ☐
5) GORD + hiatus hernia	M ☐	M ☐	I ☐	I ☐	I ☐	M ☐
6) Oesophagitis	M ☐	M ☐	I ☐	I ☐	I ☐	M ☐
7) Ulcerative colitis	I ☐	M ☐	C ☐	I ☐	C ☐	I ☐
8) Crohn's disease	I ☐	M ☐	C ☐	I ☐	C ☐	I ☐
9) Malabsorption syndromes	M ☐	M ☐	I ☐	M ☐	M ☐	I ☐

Special notes:
Differences between UC and Crohn's disease

Lists:
Risk factors and management for upper GI bleed

6. Hepatobiliary + Pancreas	Epidemiology/ aetiology	Pathology	Symptoms and signs	Investigation and DDX	Management	Complications and prognosis
1) Alcoholic liver disease	C	I	C	C	C	I
2) Cirrhosis	C	I	I	I	I	I
3) Hepatitis (including viral)	I	I	I	I	I	C
4) Wilson's disease	M	S	I	M	M	M
5) Haemochromatosis	M	S	I	M	M	M
6) Primary biliary sclerosis	S	S	M	M	S	S
7) Cholangitis	I	M	I	I	I	M
8) Alpha-1 antitrypsin deficiency	S	M	M	M	S	S
9) Hepatic CA	I	M	I	I	I	I
10) Primary sclerosing cholangitis	S	M	M	M	S	S
11) Autoimmune hepatitis	M	M	M	M	S	S

Special notes:
Hepatitis viruses and their modes of transmission
The portal venous system

Lists:
Causes of ascites
Causes of hepatomegaly and splenomegaly

TABLE 13.1 *Continued*

7. Neurology	Epidemiology/ aetiology	Pathology	Symptoms and signs	Investigation and DDX	Management	Complications and prognosis
1) Stroke + TIA	I ☐	I ☐	C ☐	C ☐	C ☐	I ☐
2) Intracranial haemorrhages	I ☐	I ☐	C ☐	C ☐	C ☐	I ☐
3) Dementia (various causes)	I ☐	I ☐	I ☐	I ☐	I ☐	M ☐
4) Parkinson's disease	I ☐	M ☐	I ☐	M ☐	M ☐	M ☐
5) Myasthaenia gravis	M ☐	I ☐	I ☐	M ☐	M ☐	M ☐
6) Meningitis	I ☐	I ☐	C ☐	C ☐	C ☐	C ☐
7) Peripheral neuropathies	I ☐	I ☐	I ☐	I ☐	M ☐	M ☐
8) Epilepsy	I ☐	I ☐	C ☐	C ☐	C ☐	I ☐
9) Multiple sclerosis	I ☐	M ☐	I ☐	I ☐	I ☐	I ☐
10) Motor neurone disease	M ☐	M ☐	I ☐	M ☐	M ☐	M ☐
11) Neurofibromatosis	M ☐	M ☐	M ☐	M ☐	S ☐	M ☐

Special notes:
Cranial nerves and their lesions
Autonomic neuropathies
Peripheral neuropathies
Mononeuropathies including individual nerve lesions, eg ulnar nerve, radial nerve

Lists:
Causes of upper and lower motor neurone lesions

8. Rheumatology	Epidemiology/ aetiology	Pathology	Symptoms and signs	Investigation and DDX	Management	Complications and prognosis
1) Rheumatoid arthritis	M ☐	M ☐	I ☐	I ☐	I ☐	I ☐
2) Systemic lupus erythematosus	M ☐	I ☐	I ☐	I ☐	I ☐	I ☐
3) Psoriasis	M ☐	M ☐	I ☐	I ☐	I ☐	M ☐
4) Septic arthritis	I ☐	I ☐	C ☐	C ☐	C ☐	I ☐
5) Gout	I ☐	M ☐	I ☐	I ☐	I ☐	M ☐
6) Pseudogout	I ☐	M ☐	I ☐	I ☐	I ☐	M ☐
7) Sjogren's syndrome	S ☐	S ☐	M ☐	M ☐	M ☐	M ☐
8) Seronegative arthiritides	M ☐	M ☐	I ☐	I ☐	M ☐	M ☐
9) Osteoarthritis	I ☐	I ☐	C ☐	C ☐	C ☐	I ☐
10) Vasculitides	M ☐	M ☐	M ☐	I ☐	M ☐	M ☐

Special notes:
Types of auto-antibodies and their involvement in disease

Lists:
Typical signs of rheumatoid versus osteoarthritis, types of seronegative arthritis, extra-articular manifestations of rheumatoid arthritis

TABLE 13.1 *Continued*

9. Haematology	Epidemiology/aetiology	Pathology	Symptoms and signs	Investigation and DDX	Management	Complications and prognosis
1) Neutropaenic sepsis	M	I	C	C	C	C
2) Leukaemias	M	I	I	I	I	I
3) Lymphomas	M	I	I	I	I	I
4) Anaemias	I	C	I	I	I	I
5) Bleeding disorders	I	I	I	I	I	M
6) Myeloproliferative disorders	M	M	M	M	S	M
7) Amylodosis	M	M	I	S	S	M
8) Multiple myeloma	M	I	I	I	I	I
9) Clotting disorders	I	I	I	I	M	M

Special notes:
First-line treatment of neutropenic sepsis
Management of over-Warfarinization

Lists:
Most common causes of anaemia

The surgical sample curriculum

We have not included the special notes and lists in this portion of the book, as these are specifically covered in the surgical section of Chapter 2.

TABLE 13.2 The surgical sample curriculum

	Epidemiology/ aetiology	Pathology	Symptoms and signs	Investigation and DDX	Management	Complications and prognosis
(1) Oesophageal						
1. Oesophageal cancer	I	I	I	I	I	I
2. Achalasia	M	M	I	I	M	M
3. Perforation of the oesophagus	M	M	I	M	I	I
4. Gastro-oesophageal reflux disease	I	I	I	I	I	I
5. Hiatus hernia	M	M	M	M	M	M
6. Pharyngeal pouch	S	S	M	M	M	S
(2) Gastric						
1. Gastric cancer	I	I	I	I	I	I
2. Peptic ulcer disease	I	I	I	I	I	I
3. Gastro-intestinal stromal tumour	M	S	M	M	M	M
4. Zollinger–Ellison disease	S	M	M	M	S	S

TABLE 13.2 *Continued*

(3) Small bowel	Epidemiology/aetiology	Pathology	Symptoms and signs	Investigation and DDX	Management	Complications and prognosis
1. Acute appendicitis	C	I	C	C	C	I
2. Meckel's diverticulum	M	M	M	M	M	M
3. Cancers of the small bowel	M	M	I	I	I	M
4. Obstruction of the small bowel	I	I	C	C	C	I
5. Intussusception	M	S	M	M	M	M
(4) Colorectal						
1. Colorectal cancer	C	I	C	C	C	C
2. Diverticular disease	I	I	I	I	I	I
3. Inflammatory bowel disease	I	I	C	C	I	I
4. Haemorrhoids	M	S	M	M	I	M
5. Anal fissure	M	M	I	M	I	M
6. Intestinal obstruction + volvulus	I	I	C	C	C	C
7. Lower GI bleed	I	I	C	C	C	I
8. Ischaemic bowel	M	M	C	C	I	I

	Epidemiology/ aetiology	Pathology	Symptoms and signs	Investigation and DDX	Management	Complications and prognosis
(5) Hepato-biliary + pancreas						
1. Pancreatic cancer	I	I	I	I	I	I
2. Pancreatitis	I	C	C	C	C	C
3. Gallstones – cholecystitis, gallstone ileus, mucocoele	I	C	I	I	I	I
4. Biliary colic	M	I	I	I	I	I
5. Cholangiocarcinoma	M	M	M	M	M	M
(6) Vascular						
1. Peripheral vascular disease	I	I	C	I	C	I
2. Aortic aneurysm	I	I	I	I	I	I
3. Venous disease	M	M	I	I	I	M
4. Carotid artery disease	I	M	I	I	I	M
5. Arterio-venous fistula	M	S	M	M	M	M
(7) Breast + endocrine						
1. Carcinoma of the breast	C	C	C	C	C	C
2. Benign breast disease	M	M	I	I	I	M
3. Thyroid disease	M	I	I	I	I	I
4. Parathyroid disease	M	M	I	I	M	I
5. Pituitary tumours	M	M	I	M	M	I

TABLE 13.2 *Continued*

(8) General surgery	Epidemiology/ aetiology	Pathology	Symptoms and signs	Investigation and DDX	Management	Complications and prognosis
1. Acute abdomen	C	C	C	C	C	C
2. Hernia	M	I	C	C	I	I
3. Lumps and bumps	M	M	I	I	I	M
4. Pilonidal sinus	S	S	M	M	M	S
(9) Urology						
Testicular tortion	M	M	C	C	I	M
Urinary retention	I	M	I	I	I	I
Bladder CA	I	I	M	I	I	I
Prostate CA + BPH	I	M	I	I	I	I
Renal calculi	I	I	I	I	I	M
Renal transplant	I	M	C	M	I	I

(10) Miscellaneous

A. Operative management of diabetic patient

B. Pre-operative assessment and complications of surgery

C. Fluid balance

D. GI bleeds

E. Orthopaedics, joint replacement, fractures, neck of femur, long bones, scaphoid, vertebra, Colles, Smith's, Monteggia, Galeazzi, fracture types

Summary

- The sample curriculum gives an idea of what is required to pass medical school finals from the knowledge perspective.

- It is a consensus document; please check for regional variations at your medical school.

- Nevertheless it should be a reasonable reflection of the depth and level to which you need to know the core conditions in order to pass medical school finals.

- Treat this document as a tool to help you in your revision planning.

- In particular, it is useful for performing for memory audit (see Chapter 11).

CHAPTER 14

Book reviews

This chapter aims to describe the diverse range of written resources for medical school finals students. There may be some books which are not listed here which are also great references – however, we have focused on the list of books which are commonly used by the students we have taught or consulted, to give an idea of the most popular books amongst medical finalists.

Each title is accompanied by a price, description and an idea of what purpose it should be used for. Please bear in mind that some books may suit some learning styles more than others, and therefore we strongly recommend that before purchasing any book you browse through it first to ensure you are happy with it. You should appraise not only the actual content, but also the layout, font, text size and general tone as it is often these factors which dictate whether you will still be using it a month onwards. Many universities, as well as teaching hospitals, will have extensive libraries with many of the titles available for borrowing; do take full advantage of this. At the beginning of your specialty attachments, try to visit the library on the first day to find and secure useful resources. However, in the melee before finals, there will undoubtably be a rush on these books, so to avoid being left in a position of not having the ideal resources available for your revision, you may wish to consider some careful purchases.

Do not be tempted into rash purchases in the immediate run-up to finals; you will spend valuable time navigating through a new book and getting used to the format. Instead, try to plan ahead. For your main references, medical, surgical and clinical examinations, you should try to pick your choice early on in the year. By the time you get to finals, your books should have a well-worn spine, highlights, annotations and labels. You will find that the consistency that comes with such practice plays an important role in your performance.

Selection of subspecialty books is a different matter, and some students feel that they manage well with lecture notes, handouts and notes made from reading during their attachment. You may wish to supplement these with library loans or purchases of key books; and we have selected books which are particularly appropriate for medical school finals in our reviews. There are many specialty books designed for specialist trainees and postgraduate exams, but the depth may be too much and they may end up being counterproductive by taking away focus from the range of other subjects to cover.

The books are reviewed in the following categories:

Clinical examination skills references

Medical references

Surgical references

Specialties

Paediatrics, psychiatry, dermatology

Clinical examination skills references

This category of books is for specific use for your physical examinations OSCE stations. Do note that these are all reasonably expensive and therefore it can be preferable to obtain one from your university or hospital library. However, in the run-up to exams these tend to be very popular and many students like to make a purchase in order to have it readily available at all times. Our advice is generally to shop around and see which book suits your own learning style as well as price range. Once you settle on a book, stick to that one for your clinical examination needs to help your own consistency of performance.

Remember the advice from the OSCE chapters (5 and 6), including the fact that there is no sequence that will please every single consultant, and developing a fluid, competent and comprehensive examination with confident presentation will allow you to pass medical school finals. We have covered many of the issues which are *not* included in these reference texts, in particular common pitfalls of students. Therefore, in preparing for finals, using the clinical examinations skills reference book in conjunction with the OSCE sections of this book will allow you to cover both the theoretical and practical aspects of the exam.

Macleod's Clinical Examination

By Graham Douglas, Fiona Nicol, Colin Robertson

ISBN 0443068488, Churchill Livingstone; 12th edition (June 2009)

RRP £40.99

Comprehensive covering of the major OSCE stations you may expect from finals, in a user-friendly set-up. This book is particularly good for grouping clinical findings into different conditions to aid learning. This approach aids in associating what you see in a clinical patient with the theoretical possibilities, and encourages you to generate differential diagnoses. The text is quite small and you may wish to see if this suits you. However, there are many boxes breaking up the text, which make it easier to digest.

Clinical Examination: A Systematic Guide to Physical Diagnosis

By Nicholas J Talley, Simon O'Connor

ISBN 0729539059 Churchill Livingstone; 6th edition (December 2009)

RRP £47.99

This book presents the OSCE examinations in a very accessible manner, with a large font size and a good range of both pictures and photos. The text content is more prose-heavy compared to the other clinical examinations references which make more use of boxes and tables. It is suited to students who want to read a lot in depth into each examination, but you may find that you need to condense this information into a standard OSCE routine to stick to timing for each station.

Clinical Examination

By Owen Epstein, G David Perkin, John Cookson, Ian S Watt, Roby Rakhit, Andrew W Robins, Graham A W Hornett

ISBN 0723434549 Mosby; 4th edition (July 2008)

RRP £48.99

The third of the large examination references in the same price range as the previous two. This book has the familiar feel of the popular A-level and GCSE subject revision guides; very user friendly, easy to read and clear. It is less focused on big lists and exhaustive tables of differential diagnoses than other OSCE references in its category. Students may find this well suited for the run-up to medical finals revision as it is easy to identify what the core processes and essential conditions are, without sifting through too much fine detail.

Medical Short Cases for Medical Students (paperback)

By Bob Ryder, Afzal Mir, Anne Freeman

ISBN 0632057297 Wiley-Blackwell (December 2000)

RRP £23.99

This is another good offering with a useful spectrum of visual aids for learning. One unique feature of this book is a sample presentation of each condition, along with common cases and examples. This will be helpful when thinking about exam performance on the day, and how to deliver and sum up your findings in a slick, concise manner.

Clinical skills: Oxford Core Text
By Naill Cox and T A Roper
ISBN 0192628747 OUP Oxford (March 2005)
RRP £30.99

This examinations reference seems to be quite plain on the outside, but covers all aspects of clinical skills and is substantially cheaper than some of the other books in this category. It also possesses some unique features such as phonetic guides to help with your verbal presentation, and numbered sequential examinations to aid memory. Furthermore, it has case problems as examples of what may come up in an examination. It is fairly prose-heavy and may be suited for those who are not so keen on tabulated data.

Medical references

This category of books can be usefully divided up into two subgroups. The first is the so-called 'Big Three' – named both for their size as well as notoriety. These are Kumar and Clark, Davidson's, and Harrison's, and will occupy significant space on any medical student's shelf. The key feature of these books is that the information contained will be *more* than that required to pass medical school finals, and in fact can be used up to postgraduate examination level. Therefore it is important to use these books carefully, and treat them as references rather than spending an eternity learning the minutiae contained within. You may wish to consider using these books with the sample curriculum (Chapter 13) in order to gauge which sections to read in depth, and which ones to focus more on concepts than details.

The second subgroup is the compact medical references, and there is significant diversity within this group. We recommend looking carefully at the options here, as they will suit different learning styles, but there are some real learning gems to be found.

Large reference texts

Davidson's Principles and Practice of Medicine;
with *student consult* online access
By Nicki R Colledge, Brian R Walker, Stuart H Ralston
ISBN 0702030856 Churchill Livingstone; 21st edition (March 2010)
RRP £47.99

Kumar and Clark Clinical Medicine
By Parveen Kumar, Michael Clark
ISBN 0702027634 Saunders Ltd; 6th edition (August 2005)
RRP £46.99

Harrison's Principles of Internal Medicine, 17th edition
By Anthony S Fauci, Eugene Braunwald, Dennis L Kasper, Stephen L Hauser, Dan L Longo, J Larry Jameson, Joseph Loscalzo
ISBN 0071466339 McGraw-Hill Medical; 17th edition (March 2008)
RRP £134.99

The three large main medical references listed above are vast texts, and more than fully comprehensive in terms of content for medical school finals – in fact, they most certainly contain more knowledge than you need in order to pass. In reading through them ourselves, and consulting with current students and graduates, it has been very difficult to pick between these excellent books. Feedback from the student body is that Harrison's is the less commonly owned of the three, due to its large price tag, but many students do not own one of these books and rely on library access. The bottom line is that you should read through some chapters of each and see which style suits you and you can feel confident that all of them are well organized and complete for your learning needs should you choose one.

Oxford Handbook of Clinical Medicine
By Murray Longmore, Ian Wilkinson, Edward Davidson, Alexander Foulkes, Ahmad Mafi
ISBN 0199232172 OUP Oxford; 8th edition (February 2010)
RRP £24.95
This book is often seen symbiotically attached to junior doctors and senior students on the wards, and is colloquially known as the 'Cheese and Onion' due to its green and yellow colour. It is probably reasonable to state that the pure knowledge contained within this book is enough to pass finals if you know all of it: an astonishing claim given its small size. It is a highly dense list-based set-up, well organized with clear explanations of conditions and management. It may not suit those students who do not like lists, and prefer more prose. We recommend all students to spend some time with it in the bookshop, if only to decide whether it is for you or not; if you do like it, it will fast become a book that you refer to every day for your final year of medical school.

Crash Course: General Medicine
By Robert Parker, Asheesh Sharma, Daniel Horton-Szar
ISBN 0723434611 Mosby; 3rd edition (June 2008)
RRP £32.99
The Crash Course series as a whole has a tendency to divide students. It presents the information clearly, and makes good use of diagrams, boxes and key points. It also has useful examination-specific tools such as sample MCQs. You may need to use this in conjunction with another reference text to reach the required depth of knowledge.

Medicine at a Glance

By Patrick Davey

ISBN 140518616X Wiley-Blackwell; 3rd edition (January 2010)

RRP £31.99

This book has a friendly style of presentation, and with its use of diagrams and easy-on-the-eye fonts, it is a pleasure to read. It is particularly good at explaining concepts in medicine which are not always easy to follow in other books. It is probably best compared to the Big Three above, in the sense of having a big book feel with small book content, and is probably enough to pass you in finals, although you may wish to supplement certain areas with other reference texts. This book may be highly suitable for some learners, particularly visual learners, whereas other learners may not like this style. We recommend that you spend some time assessing this book for compatibility with your own learning needs.

Surgical references

Surgical Talk: Revision in Surgery

By Andrew Goldberg, Gerald Stansby

ISBN 1860944949 Imperial College Press; 2nd revised edition (February 2005)

RRP £31.00

This book, comparable to the 'Cheese and Onion' in terms of ubiquity, is proclaimed as an excellent surgical book by students and graduates alike. It is very different from the Oxford handbook as it is almost fully prose, does not make heavy use of lists and tables, and makes only limited use of diagrams. However, it is fantastic prose, which makes the book very readable, containing a good depth of knowledge. It also helpfully covers other more specialist topics such as common orthopaedic fractures and the clinical anatomy of hernias.

Browse's Introduction to the Symptoms and Signs of Surgical Disease

By John Black, William Thomas, Kevin Burnand, Sir Norman Browse

ISBN 034081571X Hodder Arnold; 4th edition (July 2005)

RRP £29.99

A fantastic resource of clinical signs packed with lots of pictures and clear diagrams. Emphasis is on history and examination, so if you want to learn the management of surgical conditions, dip into another book. Examination findings are broken up into small sections just as you would find them in real life. If you don't want to read it all the way through, it is still well worth skimming through the pictures and photographs as it may be your only chance to see certain conditions which are commonly featured in finals yet rarely seen on the wards: for example, ruptured biceps tendon, skin lumps and bumps and Charcot joints.

Surgical section of the Oxford Handbook of Clinical Medicine

By Murray Longmore, Ian Wilkinson, Edward Davidson, Alexander Foulkes, Ahmad Mafi

ISBN 0199232172 OUP Oxford; 8th edition (February 2010)

RRP £24.95

Hugely underrated, this relatively small section covers many of the main surgical conditions, with a concise summary of the important points. Clear diagrams and images help to explain key anatomical areas. Excellent concise coverage of pain control, postoperative complications, blood transfusions, nutritional support and the diabetic patient undergoing surgery.

Lecture Notes: General Surgery (paperback)

By Harold Ellis, Roy Calne, Christopher Watson

ISBN 1405139110 Wiley-Blackwell; 11th edition (September 2006)

This book is unlike many in the same series, in that it is littered with attractive and useful illustrations to explain and reinforce key surgical concepts, and makes the information readily digestible. This, coupled with the lectures notes series strength of content and organization, makes it a great book when revising for medical school finals.

Specialty references

Purchasing a book for the smaller specialties is a different proposition from purchasing a core OSCE, medical or surgical book, for several reasons. First, it is important to assess the depth of knowledge required for medical finals, as specialties books range from those which are barely sufficient to pass, to those which are references for senior specialist registrars of that discipline. Second, while core medical and surgical books retain their usefulness throughout your career, particularly in the junior years, a book on a specialty may be much less relevant .

Nevertheless, you may find key books are excellent for your revision purposes, and you may wish to own a single 'core' specialty book for each discipline to focus your study efforts. This chapter points you towards options which are particularly suited for the medical school finals level. Some successful students have started their revision in the specialties early, and made notes from library accessed books; In conjunction with lecture handouts, clerked cases and notes from teachings on specialty placements, they managed to bypass the need to acquire a book for each specialty. Other students have told us that when they left revision of these topics until later, they found that specialties books were life-savers which allowed them to acquire the knowledge in that field rapidly and in an organized fashion.

We recommend reading the specialties chapter in this volume (Chapter 2) in order to prepare for this element of your finals exam early, and give it due care and attention during your placements. The books listed here should be treated as recommended reading rather than necessarily to purchase, but particularly for those short on time, they can also be very useful in the run-up to finals.

Dermatology

Dermatology: An Illustrated Colour Text
By David Gawkrodger
ISBN 0443104212 Churchill Livingstone; 4th edition (November 2007)
RRP £33.99
This book is in a vertical column format much like a newspaper. It is set up with two pages covering each individual topic, and this works well for the level of knowledge required for medical school finals. It has good illustrations, but given the large size of the book, the photos are small.

Lecture Notes: Dermatology
By Robin Graham-Brown, Tony Burns
ISBN 1405139773 Wiley-Blackwell; 9th edition (November 2006)
RRP £24.99
This book is entirely unlike the other books in its series – which are very prose-heavy, with little in the way of visual learning aids. This book is very well broken up with excellent illustrations, and presents the information in an organized and systematic manner. We recommend looking at this book even if you weren't keen on the other Lecture Notes books.

Psychiatry

Psychiatry at a Glance
By Cornelius Katona , Claudia Cooper, Mary Robertson
ISBN 1405181176 Wiley-Blackwell; 4th edition (October 2008)
RRP £23.99
Each topic in this book is presented in a schemata or flow diagram, which is fantastic for visually orientated learners. It then follows this up with prose explanations with a good level of detail, and we recommend considering this book particularly when starting your psychiatry placement, to get to grips with key concepts.

Psychiatry: An Illustrated Colour Text (paperback)
By Lesley Stevens, Ian Rodin
ISBN 0443057036 Churchill Livingstone; 2nd edition
Very memorable content with excellent use of diagrams, case histories and self-assessment questions. Also very organized and accessible. This book is therefore highly recommended, especially for those undertaking rapid revision nearer to finals.

Master Medicine: Psychiatry: A clinical core text with self-assessment

By Elspeth Guthrie, Shon Lewis

ISBN 0443062765 Churchill Livingstone (September 2002)

RRP £24.99

The book follows the appearances of others in its series – a uniform grey, coupled with good content and great self-assessment questions.

Crash Course: Psychiatry

By Julius Bourke, Matthew Castle, Daniel Horton-Szar

ISBN 072343476X Mosby; 3rd edition (July 2008)

RRP £24.99

The depth of knowledge in this book is certainly reasonable for passing finals, and coupled with the usual Crash Course strength in illustrations, key points and boxes, this book is another potential high-yield revision book prior to examinations.

Paediatrics

illustrated Textbook of Paediatrics

By Lissauer and Clayden

ISBN 0723433976 Mosby; 3rd edition (June 2007)

RRP £40.99

This user-friendly book is a commonly suggested core text and the right depth for medical students. All the core presentations and syndromes are explained concisely, with excellent use of colour, pictures and summary boxes to aid rapid recall. Emergency management of all key conditions is laid out clearly. For those keen students wishing to know more detail on particular conditions you will need to use a more advanced text, but for the general finals student this book has more than enough information to enable you to pass with distinction.

Crash Course: Paediatrics

By Shyam Bhakthavalsala, Tim Newson, Daniel Horton

ISBN 072343462X Mosby; 3rd edition (June 2008)

RRP £24.99

This is a very accessible text with good content. It has the usual section of sample questions at the back common to all in this series. The material sometimes doesn't flow easily but there are good diagrams, lists and tables.

Master Medicine: Paediatrics

By Attard-Montalto and Saha (2005)

ISBN 044307495X Churchill Livingstone; 2nd edition (November 2005)

RRP £24.99

The grey appearance detracts from the systematic layout, good prose style and memorable tables and lists. As with all of the series it has a focus on self-assessment, including questions which many students find useful in preparation for exams.

Pathology

The Robbins series on the pathologic basis of disease comes in several different-size texts depending on your enthusiasm and stamina.

Robbins and Cotran Pathologic Basis of Disease

By Vinay Kumar, Abul K. Abbas, Nelson Fausto, Jon Aster

ISBN 1416031219 Saunders; 8th edition (June 2009)

RRP £78.99

The largest is great for detailed essays and distinction candidates, as well as reference for specific in-depth topics. It may be too much to digest for use as a standard revision text on a day-to-day basis.

Robbins Basic Pathology

By Vinay Kumar, Abul K. Abbas, Nelson Fausto, Jon Aster

ISBN 1416029737 Saunders; 8th edition (May 2007)

RRP £56.99

The medium-size text is probably the most accessible, with each chapter well structured and fairly concise, yet retaining enough detail to score very highly in examinations.

Pocket Companion to Robbins and Cotran Pathologic Basis of Disease

By Richard Mitchell, Vinay Kumar, Nelson Fausto, Abul K Abbas

ISBN 0721602657 Saunders; 7th edition (February 2006)

RRP £26.59

The 'pocket' version is far bigger than most pockets, and may be enough detail for some courses depending on the format of exam and depth of knowledge required. Its portability will help on-the-go revision.

General and Systematic Pathology

By James C E Underwood, Simon S Cross

ISBN 0443068887 Churchill Livingstone; 5th edition (May 2009)

RRP £50.99

This book covers pathology with a well-woven fabric of prose, illustrations, photographs and tables, taking a systems-based approach for the basis of disease. It is comparable in content to the medium-sized Robbins, and is has a pleasantly readable feel to it. Consider this as one of your core revision books for pathology exams.

Crash Course: Pathology

By Atul Anand

ISBN 0723434220 Mosby; 3rd edition (July 2007)

RRP £29.99

Extremely accessible and worth browsing through to see if you like the way material is presented.

Obstetrics and gynaecology

Obstetrics and Gynaecology

By Lawrence Impey and Tim Child

ISBN 1405160950 Wiley-Blackwell; 3rd edition (August 2008)

RRP 35.99

This book is loved by students; so much so that examiners sometimes comment that they give similar answers in OSCE examinations as if they are singing from the same hymn sheet! This book provides core knowledge in a clear format which is ideal for rapid recall. Students like the concise style and unusually detailed summary boxes, and the material covered is an appropriate level for medical school finals.

Gynaecology by Ten Teachers

By Stanley G Clayton

ISBN 0340816627 Hodder Arnold; 18th edition (February 2006)

RRP £19.99

Although only covering the gyanaecological aspects, this book provides great depth and features case histories which are well constructed to aid comprehension. It may be a good additional text to Impey (above), particularly for distinction candidates. However, you will need a book which covers obstetrics.

Obstetrics and Gynecology: An Illustrated Colour Text

By Joan Pitkin, Alison Peattie, Brian A Magowan

ISBN 044305035X Churchill Livingstone (November 2003)

This book sets out each condition in a two-page spread, which makes it easy for students to compartmentalize their revision. It has a newspaper-style format of three columns, which some may find difficult to scan, and despite its title has relatively small photographs. May be a good resource if it suits your revision style; try to get a feel in a bookstore or library for whether you like it.

Oxford Handbook of Clinical Specialties

By Judith Collier, Murray Longmore, Tom Turmezei, Ahmad Mafi

ISBN 0199228884 OUP Oxford; 8th edition (January 2009)

RRP £24.95

We include this book in the review for O&G books but it has many of the major specialties including psychiatry, paediatrics, obstetrics and gynaecology as well as small specialties such as ophthalmology. It is very much in the style of the *Oxford Handbook of Medicine*, and if you like that, you will also find this book useful. It contains a good amount of list-based information, complemented by tables and diagrams, and its portability makes it worth considering for an all-in-one solution to carry on the wards during many of your specialty attachments.

Summary

- There is a vast range of books available to help with your medical school finals.

- Spending a little time in bookshops and libraries finding the materials that suit you is well worth the investment.

- Do not be tempted to panic-buy books a month before finals; try to plan ahead and have your books selected early in your final year.

- Specialty books can be useful aids, especially if you feel you are not given enough course materials.

- Having a core collection of well-worn, annotated books is usually the hallmark of a student destined to pass.

CHAPTER 15

Ethics and law

How to use this chapter

We understand that medical and surgical knowledge tends to be at the forefront of the agenda in revision for medical finals, and therefore this chapter is aimed as a refresher for the issues which you may have covered over the course of your years at medical school. It will allow you to maintain focus on your other subjects, while drawing together key facts and arguments to support your performance in the ethics and law element of your exams.

For each topic, we have included a skeleton essay plan of the issues you may wish to address within the context of each. Use these to refresh and consolidate your knowledge of medical ethics and law. Each plan is set out as follows: introduction, ethical issues (including four-principles analysis), legal issues, clinical issues and examples, and a conclusion.

For some ethics and law examinations, there may be some complex cases which describe these issues in clinical settings. You can still use these essay formats by identifying the main issues brought about by the case, and using the material from the essay plans in your answer. You will find it particularly useful to drop in key ethical arguments and legal references, but remember to relate these back to the case in hand.

Some medical schools set essays as the format for examinations, others have short-answer questions, and, although much less common, it is possible to see ethics and law tested through other methods such as MCQs. Remember to prepare for the specific format of your exam, but bear in mind that you can use the material present in this chapter as a basis for the factual revision.

These essay plans cannot cover every minute detail; what they do is to cover key ethical arguments and legal cases, and show how they apply to our day-to-day practice.

General ethics principles

One basic way to divide ethical problems is by looking at either the consequences of the actions or the actions themselves. **Utilitarianism** is a branch of ethics focused around consequences, and is often described as aiming for the maximum happiness for the maximum number of people. Utilitarianist thinking can be useful when looking at broad-reaching policies. However, its critics often point to the lack of protection of individuals or minorities who can be negatively affected to benefit the majority.

Deontology can be considered the opposite of this in that it looks at the actions themselves rather than the consequences. It attempts to label actions as being either universally right or wrong regardless of the outcome, and therefore has advantages in terms of clarity and transparency; however, in practice it is difficult to designate actions as entirely right or wrong.

You will also doubtlessly be familiar with the **four principles** which were proposed by Beauchamp and Childress as the main pillars of ethical reasoning in medical ethics. Respect of **autonomy** is concerned with the right for a person to make choices about their own life. **Justice** can be seen as a right to fairness and equality. **Beneficence** might be described as the duty to do good to others, and its counterpart, **non-maleficence**, as the duty not to do harm to others.

Each sample essay will look to use the four principles to analyse the ethical problems in a systematic manner.

The entire spectrum of ethical philosophies is beyond the scope of this book, or indeed a medical degree. Try to focus on applying the main principles, come to a balanced conclusion, and reflect on how this will apply to medical practice.

General legal principles

It is worth having a good understanding of the legal structure of the UK, the first major division being between **criminal** and **civil** law. Criminal law deals with serious offences and is prosecuted by the state, requiring proof beyond a reasonable doubt and trial before a jury. However, in practice most of the legal issues which will arise in medical finals will be drawn from civil law, where the burden of proof is one of 'on the balance of probabilities'. The **legislature** and **case law** are important sources of law in medical cases, and therefore we have taken pains to include the key acts and cases which you will need to refer to in order to demonstrate you understanding of the legal principles.

Knowledge of the hierarchy of courts in medical finals will be useful mainly in referring to cases which were appealed, and understanding that the judgments made at the **Supreme Court**, the highest court in the civil system, are sometimes referred to as being particularly important in changing the way we interpret the law. In the UK, we are subject to EU law which can supersede rulings from UK courts, and relevant cases will be highlighted in the individual essay plans.

Consent and capacity

We will treat consent and capacity as a single issue, but there is some degree of overlap as capacity assessment arises when a person's ability to give valid consent is in question. Therefore, you may find it useful to consider introducing issues of capacity into a consent answer, and vice versa, depending on the precise wording of your examination question.

Introduction

The importance of consent can be seen from both ethical and legal standpoints. Ethically it stems from the principle of **respect for autonomy** which suggests a right of a patient to choose what is done to them. Legally, it provides the defence for the doctor against the **crime of assault** and the civil wrong of violating a person's right to integrity of their own body. Some of the clinical issues include establishing valid consent, and problems arising when a patient is unable to consent.

Ethical issues

Respect for autonomy is a main principle. There may be times when respect for autonomy may come into conflict with the principle of **non-maleficence**, for example if a patient declines a treatment which will result in them coming to harm, but the right of a competent adult to choose what to do with their life and body does facilitate them choosing 'harm' according to their own circumstances. In terms of justice, a right to consent to treatment does not imply a right to any treatment: for example, in cases where a patient would like to have a very expensive treatment when they have not tried first-line treatments or is not a suitable candidate.

Legal issues

Any touching of another person's body without their consent can be considered assault in law, and therefore a doctor must have legal defences to allow the practice of their art; this is valid consent.

Valid consent must be **voluntary**, and therefore not coerced from the patient, or taken with undue influence from the physician. It must be **informed**, and this may include explanation of the frequently occurring and severe risks, although not every single risk must be explained. It should include all information that *any reasonable* patient would want to know. The patient must be **competent** to give consent, and in the first instance competence is presumed in all adults, except for under specific circumstances. These are stipulated in the **2005 Mental Capacity Act**, and include 'impairment or disturbance in the function of the mind or brain'. Alternatively, if this condition is not present, a patient can be considered to lack capacity if they are unable to understand, retain, use the information to come to a decision, or communicate their decision.

Capacity is specific for each treatment, and can fluctuate, and so patients must be tested for capacity for each treatment offered. If a patient is not competent, any **advance decisions** should be acted upon if valid, and if they have a nominated person with **Lasting Power of Attorney**, they should consent on behalf of the patient. Failing this, the doctor should act in the **best interests** of the patient, taking into account the social, physical and emotional considerations of the patient. They may wish to consult family and close friends, but their opinions are not binding; the doctor must come to a balanced conclusion and act.

In the case of children under the age of 16, they are presumed to be not competent and therefore their parent or legal guardian is able to give consent as a proxy. However, a child can be demonstrated to be 'Gillick competent', a term which stems from the case of **Gillick v West Norfolk and Wisbech Area Health Authority [1985]**, where a mother challenged the actions of a GP who prescribed the oral contraceptive pill to her underage daughter without her mother's consent. This case established that children above 16 years of age but below 18 are presumed competent by legislature: the **Family Law Reform Act 1969**. However, in cases of *refusal* of treatment, parents can supersede their refusal if they are seen to be acting in the best interests of the child. Note that the inverse is not true – a parent cannot refuse a treatment that their child of this age has consented to.

Clinical issues

The degree of consent should mirror the severity of the intervention being offered by the doctor. For example, for simple phlebotomy, implied consent can be assumed when a patient rolls up their sleeve and offers their arm after being asked. In cases of intimate examinations, express verbal consent should be taken, and this should be transcribed into the medical notes, which are themselves a legal document which can aid a doctor's defence. In surgery, express written consent, with careful notation of the risks which have been explained, is necessary, as the degree of severity of the intervention is far higher.

Conclusion

Ethically, the principle of autonomy trumps all when we are dealing with a person's choices about their life and body, particularly in this case when their decisions will not directly adversely affect others. Legally, awareness of the legislature surrounding valid consent and capacity determine our defence against the crime of assault. In practice, consent can be implied or expressed, but the principles of valid consent should guide our behaviour when offering treatments to patients.

Confidentiality

Introduction

Confidentiality can be considered as the duty not to reveal information regarding a patient. There are several legal requirements of maintaining confidentiality both in common law and legislature. In clinical practice, there are occasions where confidentiality is breached in order to optimize patient care.

Ethical issues

The principle of non-maleficence plays an important role in confidentiality – information gleaned from patient consultations or records has the potential to harm them if released, and this can be through stigma of a disease. Respect for a person's autonomy includes keeping their private activities in the private domain. There is an element of justice involved; if you breach confidentiality with one patient, it can affect the way the population views the safety of their information with doctors, and other patients may become less trusting of doctors and therefore volunteer less information. This could lead to poorer treatment and therefore harm to the general populace.

On the other hand, justice can sometimes require that the protection of the general public comes above that of the privacy of the individual, particular in the cases of breaching confidentiality to prevent harm. This is a utilitarianist action as it considers the needs of the many above the needs of the individual.

Legal issues

A doctor has several legal obligations to maintain confidentiality, starting with a contractual obligation with NHS Trusts in the UK, and breaches of this can lead to disciplinary proceedings or dismissal. In terms of legislation, the **Data Protection Act 1988** requires that practitioners store data that they require for the purpose stated, only as long as it is needed. Furthermore, under the **Human Rights Act 1998**, a right to 'private and family life' also requires confidentiality in doctors.

The **GMC** is a regulatory body for doctors, and its powers to caution or strike off doctors provide an important control in the regulation of confidentiality in addition to the law, and its policies are stipulated in GMC guidance on practice.

However, there are some specific circumstances where confidentiality can be breached legally. First, if a patient gives **express consent** to reveal confidential information, then a doctor can do so. There are a number of circumstances under which you must disclose information, which include:

Terrorism Act;

Road Traffic Act – the DVLA must be informed of notifiable conditions such as epilepsy;

Infectious Diseases Act – certain notifiable infectious diseases must be disclosed;

Prevent harm to patient or others;

To prevent a serious crime (murder, rape, kidnapping).

Clinical issues

In the workplace, we will often share information with colleagues or members of the MDT in order to collaborate in patient care – even though express consent to disclose has not been given. This is not a licence to broadcast information, and the principles of confidentiality state that this type of disclosure should only occur when necessary and relevant, and only regarding information which is necessary for the collaboration.

Conclusion

Ethically and legally, there is an overarching responsibility to maintain confidentiality, but there are also obligations to disclose confidential information under specific circumstances, which generally concern the welfare of others. Clinically, the principles of confidentiality should guide our practice whether consent to disclose is express or implied.

Euthanasia

Introduction

Euthanasia is a concept which surrounds palliative medicine: the active killing of a patient upon their request. While illegal in this country, there are other countries which allow it and therefore both the ethical and legal debates are important.

Ethical issues

Utilitarianist arguments focus on the outcomes of actions, and therefore there is less of a distinction drawn between omissions and acts. From this perspective, euthanasia and withdrawal of treatment might be equally beneficial to the individual and society, and thereby equally defensible. **Deontological** ethics look at the actions themselves and therefore active processes are more negative than passive ones by their very nature. Under this school of thought, allowing someone to refuse a treatment is less of a problem than taking steps to end their life.

Under the four principles, the two conflicting axes revolve around **beneficence** and **non-maleficence**, as it is difficult to reconcile whether ending a patient's life is doing good for them, or indeed whether it constitutes harm. Respect for autonomy hints towards respecting a patient's wishes to die, but again it conflicts with justice as we could be endangering others by devaluing human life and opening the door to further situations where active killing of patients is allowed. The so-called 'slippery slope' argument is often misunderstood, and contains more subtle elements than simply forcing patients to choose death; if we imagine euthanasia becoming commonplace, there may be psychological impacts on the elderly or disabled, who might feel that they don't want to burden society and therefore have a subconscious pressure to choose euthanasia.

Legal issues

Under the Suicide Act 1961, suicide is no longer illegal and therefore failed attempts at suicide would no longer be subject to legal repercussions. However, this act also criminalizes assisting suicide, and forms the legal basis for prosecution of those involved in euthanasia.

The 'doctrine of double effect' surrounds grey areas such as the use of morphine in high doses for palliation, but with a result of harm and eventually death of the patient. The basis of this is whether harm or help is intended, and if pain relief is the primary goal, then various side effects, including the shortening of life, are permissible, provided the patient has given adequate consent. This is not the same as intending to harm a patient using a substance which is also a painkiller, and it should be clear that the underlying motivation is one of palliation rather than anything else, in order for this doctrine to be valid.

Clinical issues

In practice, euthanasia remains illegal in the UK. Excellence in palliative care should help to reduce the need for euthanasia by decreasing the burden of symptoms on the patient. Nevertheless, media publicity of euthanasia 'centres' in Europe offer a possibility to patients to travel abroad to have euthanasia provided in countries such as Holland and Switzerland. As the Suicide Act 1961 states that 'A person who aids, abets, counsels or procures the suicide of another, or an attempt by another to commit suicide' is guilty of an offence, you are not legally able to provide information on this subject.

Resource allocation

Introduction

There are two main resource allocation issues which can occur in finals, the first being how we as a profession can choose between expensive treatments for limited numbers of people and cheaper interventions which may be less effective. The second is the 'blame' debate: should we be treating those who are responsible for the conditions they find themselves in?

Ethical issues

Utilitarianist arguments for treatment allocation form a simple, almost mathematical solution to this problem: we should optimize the amount of happiness or benefit to the population by using those treatments which have the **most efficient cost–benefit ratio**, in a system of limited resources. Deontologists, however, might deem that there is a reason why some should be given treatments rather than others, and the **action of denying** a patient an expensive treatment could be wrong, depending on the circumstances.

Using the four principles, beneficence in trying to do good to the patients you are treating can come into conflict with the principle of justice, where you may be denying many others access to treatment by undertaking an expensive treatment on your own. Autonomy, the right for us to choose our own healthcare product, would not be limited in a free market economy where we can purchase our own medicals, and indeed this is true to a certain extent in private medicine. Nevertheless, in the UK where most of the healthcare provision is provided by the state, we must take care to balance the needs of individuals with those of the health of the nation.

Legal issues

Article 2 of The Human Rights Act 1998 states that we have a 'right to life', and legal questions have been raised about whether this means we are being denied this right if we are not allocated treatments. However, rulings such as those in the case of *R v Swindon NHS Primary Care Trust 2006* showed that a government would only be denying a person's right to life if they denied a patient treatment that they had otherwise made available to the rest of the population. In this case Ann-Marie Rogers was denied Herceptin, a very expensive medication, and this was deemed legal as it was not generally available to all patients with her condition.

In UK law, in *R v Cambridge HA ex p B*, it was ruled that the healthcare providers should be the ones to make the rationing and allocation decisions rather than the courts, as they are better placed to do so and it is in fact their responsibility. However, they must be able to demonstrate reasonable and consistent justification for their actions, and should not make any decisions on gender, race or religious differences.

Clinical issues

More expensive medications are often limited and require approval by a board in order to be given, and this means a great deal of paperwork for practising doctors. Although we may feel sympathetic to the patient at hand, it is important to remain objective in the submission of proposals for treatment allocation. Having uniform standards of comparison, including factors such as prognosis, is important for all patients, including your own, to be treated fairly.

Conclusion

The balance between providing treatments for the individual and the community has both an ethical and a legal basis, and logical, non-discriminatory analysis forms the backbone for the justification of resource allocation in both cases.

Negligence

Introduction

Negligence is one of the rare issues that are almost entirely legal in nature. It falls under the umbrella of Tort law, which is civil rather than criminal, and therefore the burden of proof is 'on the balance of probabilities' rather than 'beyond reasonable doubt'.

It is very rare to have a criminal charge brought about by negligence, and in such cases the doctor must be shown to have exhibited 'reckless' behaviour with regards to a patient's health and safety. Negligence under Tort law has three specific conditions which need to be met.

Legal issues

These are:

1) The doctor owed the patient a duty of care. In practice, this is always the case when you are the treating doctor of the patient. It also occurs to patients whom you are treating in other emergency circumstances, eg in an aeroplane or on the street.

2) The doctor was in breach of his duty of care. Doctors must provide an appropriate standard of care to patients.The standard of care required is stipulated in case law by *Bolam v Friern 1957*, during which it was deemed that a 'A doctor is not guilty of negligence if he has acted in accordance with practice accepted as proper by a responsible body of medical men skilled in that particular art.' This is known as the Bolam test, and essentially means that having a responsible body of doctors who would have acted in a similar fashion would be a valid defence for a doctor. However, this was limited by *Bolitho v City and Hackney Health Authority 1997*, which states that this kind of defence does not tolerate any manner of practice; rather that in addition to showing that a responsible body of practitioners would also act in this manner, it must be amenable to logical analysis.

3) Harm was suffered as a result of the breach of duty. This can often be the most difficult element to prove, as medically even a breach of duty may not have been the direct cause of death or harm. Furthermore, patients often have multiple pathologies and it may not be the case that harm was suffered as a result of the doctor's action.

Clinical issues

In practice, individual doctors are covered by indemnity with a defence union, predominantly the MDU or MPS in this country. In areas when they are unsure, they can consult these organizations by telephone in the first instance, and in hospital medicine can also draw upon the advice of a hospital legal team.

Conclusion

Negligence is predominantly a legal issue which has strict conditions which must be met for a doctor to be found negligent. In practice, doctors should ensure that they are practising in accordance with a body of responsible doctors, and so following NICE, national society or hospital guidelines offers a strong position to base one's actions. However, this should not blind doctors to following defensive protocol, and in particular using the wrong guidelines for a different condition, or in the wrong circumstances, can still give rise to a claim of negligence.

Abortion

Ethical issues

The main conflict in the ethics of abortion revolve around the rights of the mother versus those of the foetus. In terms of non-maleficence, we have a duty not to do harm to humans; however, the status of the foetus as a potential life, fully blown human life, or simple ball of cells, is one which is in debate. The characteristics which are debated include, but are not limited to, consciousness, the ability to feel pain, the potential to grow into an adult, or the potential to survive outside the womb unaided. There are a number of religions which are opposed to abortion, but on closer analysis the argument boils down to whether the foetus is human or not. In some religions, the foetus is considered equivalent to a full human at the point of conception, whereas others consider this to occur as late as parturition,

Some argue that if a foetus will be born with serious disabilities, it is better for it not to live rather than suffer this. While this seems a simple enough argument, we must remember that we are comparing two conditions: living with a serious handicap, or not living at all, and it is difficult to say that one of these situations is obviously better than the other, such that we should always intervene.

Other arguments lie along the lines of autonomy, and these may be better developed. The mother, being a fully developed human, has a right to choose what happens with regards to her body. The fact that there is a foetus growing inside her does not mean she should be forced to be a prisoner to its usage of her body, simply because it cannot survive without her. The mother may choose to allow the foetus to use her body in such a way, but she should have the choice over whether it does or does not.

Legal issues

The Abortion Act 1967 stipulates the basis for legal terminations of pregancy. Points to note:

- The pregnancy must be terminated by a medical practitioner.
- There must be two practitioners who are of the opinion that the termination of pregnancy is required for one of the reasons below:
  - <24 weeks and continuance of the pregnancy would involve risk greater than if the pregnancy were terminated, of injury to the physical or mental health of the pregnant woman or any existing children of her family;
  - Termination necessary to prevent grave permanent injury to the physical or mental health of the pregnant woman;
  - Continuance of the pregnancy would involve risk to the life of the pregnant woman, greater than if the pregnancy were terminated;
  - Substantial risk that the child would suffer from such physical or mental abnormalities as to be seriously handicapped;
  - In determining whether the continuance of a pregnancy would involve such risk of injury to health ... account may be taken of the pregnant woman's actual or reasonably foreseeable environment.

These conditions form the legal basis for termination of pregnancy, and in practice the first reason listed above is very easily applicable, as carrying of a pregnancy to term will always be a greater risk to health than to have an abortion. It also makes unlicensed abortions ('back-alley' abortions), illegal.

Clinical issues

Under the Abortion Act 1967, medical practitioners are allowed to have a conscientious objection, and are not obliged to perform the duties authorized by the Act. However, they cannot actively deny a patient access to treatment based on this objection. This legal position takes into account the various ethical positions that doctors may hold, while still placing the patient, quite rightly, at the forefront of healthcare.

Conclusion

Ethically, abortion is a service provided by the medical community which respects the right of women to their own body, and the rights of a fully developed human can be seen to supersede the rights of the unborn child, which are more subject to controversy. Legally, it must be performed by medical practitioners under strict conditions, but in practice the conditions are evident in almost all cases before the 24-week threshold.

Rapid access legal cases

Consent and capacity:

2005 Mental Capacity Act – stipulates conditions of capacity.

Gillick v West Norfolk and Wisbech Area Health Authority 1985 – Gillick competence.

Family Law Reform Act 1969 – parents can accept, but not refuse, a treatment for their child.

Confidentiality:

Data Protection Act 1988 – stipulates our duties in confidentiality of data.

The Human Rights Act 1998 – right to private and family life.

Terrorism Act – serious crime, including suspected terrorism, should be reported.

Road traffic Act – the DVLA must be informed of notifiable conditions such as epilepsy.

Infectious Diseases Act – certain notifiable infectious diseases must be disclosed.

Euthanasia:

Suicide Act 1961 – makes suicide legal, but aiding or abetting suicide illegal.

Resource allocation:

Article 2 of The Human Rights Act 1998 – only in breach if government denies treatments which are made generally available to the public.

R v Cambridge HA ex p B – healthcare authorities, not courts, should determine allocation.

Negligence:

Bolam v Friern 1957 – the Bolam test for standard of care.

Bolitho v City and Hackney Health Authority 1997 – limitations to the Bolam test.

Abortion:

Abortion Act 1967 – stipulates conditions for legal abortion.

Summary

- Ethics and law essays require a degree of preparation.

- In terms of ethics, a four-principles analysis and looking at the utilitarian–deontological spectrum should be sufficient to cover most cases.

- This is because questions require you to show comprehension and application, rather than simple recall.

- However, legal elements require factual input from cases and legislature.

- Discussion of clinical relevance is often overlooked by students, and helps to demonstrate your understanding of the topics in exams.

- Ethics and law are often neglected in the run-up to finals, but if you prepare carefully in advance, you will be able to focus on your main medical and surgical material with less distraction.